The Lay Pastoral Worker's Hospital Handbook

Tending the Spiritual Needs of Patients

Neville A. Kirkwood

morehouse

HARRISBURG • LONDON

Morehouse Publishing, P.O. Box 1321, Harrisburg, PA 17105
Morehouse Publishing, The Tower Building, 11 York Road,
London SE1 7NX
Morehouse Publishing is a Continuum imprint.

Cover design by Dana Jackson

Library of Congress Cataloging-in-Publication Data

Kirkwood, Neville A.
    The lay pastoral worker's hospital handbook : tending the spiritual needs of patients / Neville A. Kirkwood.
        p.   cm.
    Includes bibliographical references.
    ISBN 0-8192-2190-2 (pbk.)
    1. Church work with the sick.   2. Lay ministry.   I. Title.
BV4335.K567   2005
259'.411—dc22

                                                            2004027246

Printed in the United States of America

01 02 03 04 05 06 07 08 09   10 9 8 7 6 5 4 3 2 1

✦ CONTENTS ✦

An official visit by identified lay pastoral visitors has deeper significance for the denomination. In some hospitals they may have access to denominational lists through the chaplain or visiting clergy. Where a chaplaincy department is firmly established, such lists may not be available even to visiting clergy. Organization and structure of each hospital varies. All pastoral care workers should, therefore, acquaint themselves with local hospital protocol before engaging in such ministry.

Lay pastoral visitors usually identify themselves to the nursing unit manager, or the ward clerk in some institutions. The staff will then know that the patient has community pastoral support and it will probably be assumed by the staff that the patient would appreciate a call to the chaplain or visiting clergy if the patient's condition should deteriorate or there develops some special condition (such as depression, for example) which is outside the normal course of the treatment or its side effects.

Lay pastoral visitors generally are quite regular in their visits. The frequency is more readily noted when a report is made to the nursing station and staff; acquaintance with the pastoral worker often produces a warmer and more cooperative relationship. Staff who have built up confidence in the pastoral carer are likely to pass on information that may assist them in their understanding of the patient.

In most hospitals the visiting hours have been extended from 12 noon or 2:30 p.m. to 8 p.m. Pastoral visitors are advised to work within those hours for the patients' welfare. There may be hospitals where special concessions are possible for lay pastoral visits outside these hours, but it is generally wise not to abuse privileges or make special demands. Depending upon the local arrangements, the visitor reports to the parish clergy person or the denominational chaplain, whoever is responsible for visitors within the hospital.

→ CHAPTER 1 ←

The Patient's Needs

Susan Williams was involved in a road accident. With fractured legs, she was given a six weeks' sentence in hospital. I use the word "sentence" because that is what it seems like to a very mentally alert and athletically active young lady. Her netball team was leading the competition. Now she will miss the final, including the coveted trophy for her shelves.

George Arnold, fifty-two years of age, a good, honest battler, lives an ordinary quiet suburban life. He is a storeman and packer so his income does not allow for many of the luxuries of life. His teenage children, some still at school, are demanding and hard to discipline. His serious heart attack looks like forcing him to take an invalid pension. With still three years to complete his

1

house mortgage repayment, George has many concerns on his mind.

Karen Reid has the most adorable children, aged seven, five and two, and at thirty-two she should be at the prime of life. Instead, an ultrasound has shown a sizeable mass in her abdomen. Is it cancer or fibroids, or perhaps a cyst? Malignant or benign? That is her great question. Will she live to see her children through school, marriages and grandchildren? Everything has that terrible cloud of uncertainty hanging over it.

Mark Brown has been told he has leukemia, a very acute form, and the doctors warn him of the consequences if he does not have treatment. They have also stated clearly that the only option is chemotherapy, with its possible and unpredictable side effects. And even with chemotherapy there are no promises, only "maybes." To have chemotherapy or not is an extremely hard decision to make. His wife, Joyce, has always been so dependent on him; the children are married and scattered in the country and interstate.

The hours of lying in that bed are hours of loneliness and mental torture for Mark, not made any easier by his wife's holding his hand. He cannot express his feelings to her. He wants her with him yet it hurts just to see and feel her there.

John and Cheryl are elated that they have a beautiful baby daughter, after nine years of marriage and unproductive previous attempts to conceive. Their dreams have come true.

Mrs. Wilson is doing well after having bunions removed. In fact, she is enjoying being waited upon.

Young Craig has come in to have his appendix out as it has been causing him problems. He is bouncy about it, although somewhat apprehensive. The first time in hospital for him is like the mixed feelings of a first trip of white-water rafting.

Anne is in her eighties and in hospital for chronic obstructive airways disease. She is gasping for breath. Having to wear that uncomfortable oxygen mask is exhausting. Her family is not game to tell her that her daughter was killed in a road accident.

Shirley Davis's concern is not unlike Joe Ferguson's. Shirley has breast lumps and is to have a mastectomy. Joe has prostate problems and also requires surgery. Both are worried that their respective femininity and masculinity are to be excised by the surgeon's knife. They have logical explanations to the contrary but their emotions suggest otherwise.

All these individuals, along with the diabetic, asthmatic, renal, pneumonic, neurosurgical patients—and scores of other types—are the people whose bedsides you approach as a pastoral worker. They are all experiencing different needs, feelings and sensations.

As a lay pastoral worker you should always inform the hospital staff of your presence. The patient may have spoken to the staff concerning spiritual needs (or a lack of desire to have a pastoral visit). Your speaking with staff also helps them to understand the patient's support network.

SENSITIVITY

Above all else, patients need your sensitivity to their particular needs and circumstances. Pastoral workers often mistakenly consider they have an unchallengeable right to be at a bedside. On the contrary, our right to be there depends on whether the patient is comfortable with us at that time. When the patient comes to feel the need to make conversation and entertain the visitor, then the visit is a failure. The visitor is an embarrassment.

The patient is often too polite to ask you to leave. Your ready ability to assess the situation and feelings of anyone of the above types of patients is a necessary skill to be developed by you as a hospital pastoral worker. Such sensitivity, of course, comes with training and experience.

APPROPRIATENESS

Your developed powers of observation enable you to be more sensitive to the patient's condition. That ability to read and act appropriately to the unspoken will enhance the chances of your acceptance.

Mary had just been told her condition was terminal and that further treatment would not be possible. She would receive only palliative care to keep her comfortable. Mary was lying there shattered. "Mid-forties is too young to die" was the thinking behind the sad, lethargic, depressed look.

The recently retired, spritely, happy Mr. Brown, the Church pastoral visitor, bounced in and chirpily asked, "How's my bright girl today?" Mary, the patient, started to sob saying, "The doctor told me there is no more treatment possible."

"What nonsense! What would he know?" was Mr. Brown's opening salvo. "We will have you out in no time. It won't be long before you will be into your bikini and having those hilarious pool parties at your place. We can't have you losing your reputation now, can we?" All this seemed to hit the midships of Mary's emotions. Her tears flowed broken-heartedly.

"Now, there is no need to cry. Come on, dry those tears!" Mr. Brown blundered on. "You should not upset yourself too much. What would your husband think if he saw you crying like this?"

Such a type of conversation is not an isolated instance. It happens daily in any major hospital. It reeks of inappropriateness. The only thing the patient does not do is to scream out, "Get out of here, you insensitive buffoon." To be smart, or to try to be funny in the presence of a despondent and deflated patient is simply inappropriate. Considerable skill is required to appreciate when and how to promote brightness. The right times are rare and only a few people can successfully do it with an anxious, depressed patient.

A young trainee pastoral care person learned a significant lesson when reflecting to a group upon what he considered a successful pastoral encounter. This patient, Mrs. Connor, had been diagnosed as having cancer a few hours earlier and was scheduled for emergency surgery the next morning.

"When are you going for the operation?" was a suitable question to ask. It showed concern and interest. It could have been intended to see whether it was possible to visit her and pray with her before she went.

On hearing that she was scheduled for the morning, the trainee's response was inappropriate. Uttered with a smile, it was an endeavor to be bright: "So you will be first cab off the rank tomorrow." The lady was probably still in double shock; she had been told she had unsuspected cancer and then told of immediate emergency surgery. A person trying to come to grips with both blows certainly would not appreciate being compared with a cab going for a ride.

APPROPRIATE RESPONSES

Mrs. Connor would have responded positively to the visitor if she could have taken in anything he was saying, if he had said something along these lines:

"You have been hit with two hammers" or "You feel like you're dreaming and you are going to wake up and find that it's not true" or "It must seem like the rug has been pulled from under you by the doctor" or "To be told that by the doctor must be devastating."

There is not a question in any of those responses. They leave the way open for Mrs. Connor, if she is not in too great a state of shock, to start expressing what she is feeling deep inside. The door is left ajar for her to push open and share her bewilderment and shock if she feels trusting enough to do so. She is also able to let the matter rest and close the door. Sensitivity leads to appropriate responses that you should respect.

JUST TO BE

Both terminally ill Mary and Mrs. Connor were in a state of shock. Conversation would not have been acceptable. When such news is conveyed to a patient, there is a need to be quiet and try to collect thoughts, to come to grips with the situation. In such circumstances coordinated thinking is difficult. Often a multitude of concepts, people, consequences and what now may seem like vain aspirations float around in a confusing mix, with no one idea becoming firmly anchored.

The pastoral worker's conversation, however bland, may add to the turmoil going on within.

Just to be with the patient in silence is often preferable.

A young adult had a motorcycle accident and was brought in with major head injuries—suspected "brain death." For two and a half hours the doctors worked on him. I sat with his wife during that period. She was silent. The only conversation concerned periodical reports on what was happening in the emergency receiving room. After the declaration of death it became a coroner's case. The police took another hour before arriving for identification of the body. Again, in that hour, less than a hundred words passed between us.

When I escorted the wife to her car, she broke down, sobbing, thanking me for my help, support and comfort. I had sensed that all she wanted was to be alone with her thoughts in order to come to grips with what was happening. I had been content "to be" there for her. Her thoughts were interrupted only with essential information.

Sensitivity enables the pastoral worker to be the right type of support at the right time (as long or short as necessary) with as few or as many words as fit the circumstances. That is true pastoral care—"to be." Patients need to be able to find their own coping mechanisms and the carer needs to be the type of person the patient requires at each visit. To be the one who recognizes those coping needs is to be a pastoral carer.

TO SEE THE CHRIST IMAGE

Surely the most effective pastoral care person recorded in history is Jesus. His sensitive handling of each and every encounter has provided the perfect model. He astounded people, bringing comfort and peace to folks such as the woman at the well, the widow of Nain, Zaccheus, Jairus, Mary of Magdala, Mary and Martha, his tormentors at Calvary, Peter and the Emmaus disciples. (See chapter 5, "Jesus—A Theological Model.")

A person enduring hospitalization needs the care of someone like Jesus. They need to recognize a person of the Jesus mold at their bedside. That same gentle discerning touch can provide the soothing warmth and relief that was experienced by the people of Galilee and Judea so long ago. Jesus promised that his disciples would do greater things than he did after the Holy Spirit filled their lives.

The pastoral carer must be recognized as one bearing that same touch. It is this that speaks of

Jesus, not our Scripture reading or our offered prayer. Our prayers become meaningful and valued only after the Christ has been first discerned in the carer.

The best textbooks for pastoral care are the four Gospels. Studying Jesus and his attitude to each person is essential. Our minds, thoughts, lives and actions should be so filled with Jesus that, like light, we bring the Jesus image and way to the bedside. A carer becomes Christ to the patient. This is our responsibility: to be a modern-day reincarnation of Christ to the patient. Presumptuous? No! It is an awesome responsibility that emphasizes our own humanity and dependence upon Christ.

If we are diligent to know him more, our efforts to naturally model him in our lives, both within and outside the hospital, will bear fruit.

Whether patients acknowledge it or not, they need to see the Christ image and touch reflected in the pastoral care workers at the bedside. Paul suggested that we become living letters, able to be seen and read by the community around us. This should be more evident at the bedside, where people are often longing for such a sighting.

TO COMMUNICATE

Pastoral care of the sick may now be understood as something much more than a social call, more than a friendly visit, more than just a wish to cheer the patient up. A pastoral visit to the bedside should hold an aura of responsibility, not of a duty to be discharged. The first visit should never be taken as a last visit. The patient may expect from you henceforth a commitment that may mean demands on your time, energy and emotions.

The outcome of your visit is unpredictable. Some visits will be encouraging and full of blessing. Others will leave you with a sense of failure, whether that truly be the case or not. In actual fact, the assumed failure may have created such a good impression that your next appearance at the bedside will be eagerly anticipated, and the assumed "successful" visit may have actually been an absolute disaster in the patient's view! The object of your visit is to communicate. There are many ways of communication. For face-to-face encounters, the ancient Epictitus gives us a clear hint: "Nature has given to man one tongue, but two ears, that we may hear from others twice as much as we speak." The patient should be the one allowed to do most of the talking.

Joseph Zima[1] takes this up further in his chapter on "Listening." He says, "Listening involves eyes and ears." So he takes communication one step beyond Epictitus. Hearing, sight and speech are involved in communication. He develops his case by stating that listening is a complete process involving hearing, understanding, judging, storing and responding.

Ole Harlem[2] in his advice to the medical profession on dealing with patients analyzes communication as having three integral parts:

- To make known one person's thoughts or ideas to others
- To do so with as much ease and as quickly as possible
- To convey knowledge of things

He says language is abused when it fails on any of these points. When we are a hospital pastoral visitor, our role is to allow the patient or the family to communicate with us. For the pastoral scene the word "feelings" should be included in the first point above, making it thoughts, feelings or ideas.

Likewise, the third point could be rewritten: "To convey knowledge of attitudes and feelings."

Often the best communicators are children. They are able to fulfill all the above criteria. Yet we usually take little notice of them or ignore the knowledge and information they are communicating. By so doing we prove to them that we cannot be trusted with their communication. Consequently, we may see them talking with their dolls, pets, a tree or themselves in a special hideaway. This continues until they feel ready to test our trust again. Patients and their relatives need to have their confidence in us, too, as accepters of communication, to be respected and actively honored in the appropriate way.

A person's real need in hospital as elsewhere is for someone to listen to them as a fellow human being. Lake makes some significant observations:

"If present loneliness can induce neurotic anxiety, then its opposite, namely genuine company, can combat neurotic anxiety."[3] An attentive listener can put to flight an army of irrational fears. "By offering to be an attentive listener . . . we draw (the patient/relative) back into a place of safety." Any pastoral visitor who cannot listen hard and long will very quickly become irritated and fidgety. He or she will take over the conversation and the patient will become the passive, disinterested and hurting listener.

Zima identifies two components of any communication, namely:

- The content of the message—information value
- The feelings of the message—the underlying attitudes and emotions

In this he suggests that there are two strands of conversation going on in communication, one verbal and the other nonverbal. In our communication with our patient, we should be the gatherer of offered information and at the same time the identifier of the feelings that are being emitted.

Sensitive listening is hard work. It is active, not just sitting passively. Reflecting on the contents of what is being said and the feelings of the patient or relatives helps to deduce meaning. Similarly, reflecting upon these meanings helps to discern the implications.

Suppose a man has been told that he has cancer and that the only treatment is chemotherapy. The patient recalls the situation of a relative who had received chemotherapy and had long and uncomfortable side effects.

After the listener has reflected on the knowledge of the cancer, he or she reflects on the feelings to discover meaning. If the listener suggests, "You must be frightened (or some such feeling word) *because* of your relative's experience," this remark promotes further reflection.

The reason for the fear is now acknowledged. The implications of that fear must be recognized through further reflection: "You are therefore scared to agree to have the chemo." The implication of the knowledge and the feelings is that the patient is negative in attitude toward undergoing such treatment.

Simply, it may be said that sensitive listening is able to reflect content, feelings, meanings and implications. The patient knows that the communication is being heard, resulting in deeper perception of what is happening personally within and without.

It has been pointed out that listening involves the eyes as well as ears. As the patient speaks, the body posture and movements are revealing. The genuine feelings and truth that are difficult to express in words are being transmitted. This is commonly called "body language."

There is also a hearing with the third ear. Effective listening involves hearing with the first ear the words that are being said. Hearing with the second ear is hearing what the words are not saying but what the nonverbals are telegraphing. The third ear is that which discerns what the patient cannot express—maybe because the real situation is not fully understood. Relationships, loyalty, or fear may be prohibiting overt revelation. In other words, there are times when words and body language together are inadequate; that is when the third ear is required.

Reflection is the opposite of expressing an opinion. Once you have passed judgment, that is, an opinion, whether critical or favorable, it makes patients' free expression difficult. They need all the friends they can have, so they will not offend you by disagreeing with you. Even the positive and encouraging evaluations you offer make it difficult for people to talk about fears, faults or failings that may be distressing them. To reveal these or even harbor them within, in the light of your good comments, may cause the patient to develop or increase feelings of guilt. Pastoral communication's aim is to release the person from fears and guilt, not to increase them.

Two patients from the same parish objected to their minister's visits. He was uncomfortable at the bedside so he resorted to a good sprinkling of pious talk, Bible reading and prayer. He became a religious man and ceased to be a Christian.

Every pastoral worker must wait until there is a freedom to speak of holy things, a freedom which the Holy Spirit gives. Dietrich Bonhoeffer's advice[4] well applies to the bedside visit when he says that we should listen with the ears of God that we may speak the word of God. Maybe this is a fourth ear that we should develop as a pastoral worker with the hospitalized.

Thus we should not enter a hospital with a preconceived idea of the issues we want to raise with the patients. Such will pollute any effort at sincere listening. Our preoccupation will be with waiting for a suitable time to intrude our own agenda items into the conversation. Our ability to permit the patient to reflect and to discover the meaning at the back of the communication will be destroyed. Perhaps our agenda items are our own perceived concern and totally irrelevant for the patient.

After your visit it may be rewarding to evaluate your listening skills against the checklist below:

Negative

Was there any one-way conversation (the patient being the silent one)?

Were there any negative interruptions by you that changed the conversation?

Did you ignore attempts at understanding?

Did you notice your own negative emotional reactions to what was said?

Did you miss any opportunities to use reflection?

Positive

Did you encourage the patient to explore and clarify statements?

Did you use reflection effectively?

Were there few "yes"/"no" responses to interruptions?

Were there positive interpretations of what was happening?

It will pay to do such an evaluation after each significant encounter.

NOTES

1. Joseph P. Zima, *Interviewing: Key to Effective Management*, 39–58.

2. Ole K. Harlem, *Communication in Medicine: A Challenge to the Profession*, 30–32.

3. Frank Lake, *Clinical Theology: A Theological/Psychological Basis to Clinical Patoral Care*, 1–28.

4. Dietrich Bonhoelfer, *Life Together: The Classic Exploration of Faith in Community*, 99.

→ **CHAPTER 2**

The Patient In Crisis

ILLNESS IS A CRISIS

It is rare that a person is admitted to hospital without some justifiable reason. The patient has gone to the local medical officer or the hospital emergency department with certain complaints about some physical or emotional functional change. Weighing the evidence of verbal description, physical examination, obvious symptoms, X-ray and other tests, the doctor deems that there are grounds for a hospital admission. Things are not right. When the body is not performing as designed, the person is living below normal efficiency and therefore is suffering some deprivation. The sufferer is in some form of crisis. And crisis produces anxiety and uncertainty: a threat hangs over the normal living of the person, the family and maybe even a wider circle.

Illness, however mild, raises the specter of mortality. Human finiteness—the weakness and frailty of human flesh—becomes more evident. Unless a pastoral worker is able to understand some of the personal dynamics and enter into the feelings of the people being visited, the visit is of little consequence. Many times patients request that a minister or pastoral worker not come again. Without sensitivity the visitor has probably pontificated and made presumptive, even dogmatically pious pronouncements as to how the patient should react. He or she has squashed and driven inside the patient's natural emotional reactions.

In any crisis situation, such a reaction is that which is appropriate to the temperament and nature of the person to cope with the situation. It may be stunned silence, talkativeness, a questioning of God, self and others, shrinking from reality; it may be panic, tantrums, the expression of anger or self-blame. These are all coping reactions. They are right reactions for that person at that time. We must accept them as such and not judge them by the way we ourselves would react or how we think they *should* cope with the circumstances.

Elisabeth Kubler-Ross identifies them in her general classification of stages.[1] Her term "stages of death and grief" is not useful as it has been interpreted and applied differently from the way she intended. A more lucid perception of all the emotions of grief is obtained, I believe, when we speak of them as "the coping mechanisms of grief" and there are many more than Kubler-Ross's five. The question that we should hold in our minds as we observe some of these reactions around the bedside is "What is triggering off these reactions?" There are a number of different things that a patient in crisis meets that cause fear and panic to develop. We shall look at some of these fear reactions separately, recognizing that each case is different and that there may be even more types of fear and their causes than we discuss here.

SYMPTOMS

Before the patient even comes into hospital the stage has often been set for fears to snowball. The lethargic feeling that has been creeping on for months has meant curtailing some activities and even missing out on others. Maybe the resulting lack of concentration has been producing decreasing efficiency at work. The back pains that were once put down to heavy lifting are now getting worse. It is getting harder and harder to pass a stool and now there is a show of blood. Those chest pains passed off as indigestion are now accompanied by a shooting feeling down the left arm. These symptoms cannot be ignored.

The sufferer endures, however, because of fear of what the doctor might reveal. The family notices the changes. The loved one tires more readily. Or bruises very easily. Or, more quickly irritated, uncharacteristically snaps back. When asked if anything is wrong, he or she bites your head off. The symptoms are denied and put to one side. What is the basis of this denial? Is it the fear of what these signs might reveal?

The patient thus may have been beset with this fear for a considerable time before arrival at the hospital.

THE LANGUAGE OF DIAGNOSIS

The reason for the initial admission to hospital is to perform tests that are intended to identify the cause of the presenting symptoms. The language of diagnostic tests creates the major fear of the early days following admission: "We'll send you for a CT scan." "I think a liver biopsy is necessary." "An endoscopy is called for." "An electroencephalogram (EEG) is the order." "We have to give you an angiogram." New terms—new words—the patient does not know what is involved with the procedure. Often doctors do not tell the patient why a test is being done or what they are looking for. Whatever it is, it sounds ominous. Patients put on a brave front that seems like a mask, as they fob off on relatives' questions. They try to recall the stories they have heard from others about relatives who have had similar tests and later died from an incurable disease.

Unless there is denial, the tendency is to dwell on the most pessimistic interpretation of the results of the tests. Thus the second tier of fears is the mention of tests in the language of diagnosis.

The third tier, still relating to diagnosis, is added a day or two later when the doctor returns with the result. Here the powerful language of diagnosis may create severe anxiety, even panic, in the patient. Cancer, leukemia, a mass in the bowel, a cardiovascular accident, chronic obstructive airways disease, blocked arteries, stroke and so on. These are all terms that are not fully understood. Even when the doctor tries to explain what a term means, the mind is so full of dread of the worst possible consequences that the words come across as garbled sounds. *The mind absorbs only what it can bear and it may hallucinate as to the course of the disease,* or simply shift into neutral.

Where the patient cannot face the truth or adversity, the coping mechanism of denial really begins to take control. We must accept that such denial is a sanctuary to which the patient flees for shelter and protection. For the present it is a very adequate coping mechanism for the fears that the language of diagnosis has caused the stricken one. To destroy that haven prematurely is to increase a flood of those fears and drown the emotions with hopelessness and despair.

TOO MUCH TOO SOON

The patient may have been ill for some time at home waiting for the doctors to come to some conclusion. During that period he or she frequently is forming a personal opinion of what the problem is. Surprisingly, these unscientific self-diagnoses often prove to be accurate. A fact to store away in the memory is that eighty percent of terminally ill patients know of their condition before doctors tell them, according to Kubler-

Ross and others: Nevertheless, many such patients fear being told too much, too soon. Again that coping mechanism of denial comes into play allowing the mind and emotions to absorb sufficient information without breaking the spirit.

A father of two early teenagers, a fit, healthy-looking man, went for exploratory abdominal surgery. He was closed up again without anything being done. The abdominal cavity was riddled with cancer. The surgeon told him, "You have a fifty percent chance of living two years and a twenty percent chance of living five years." This wise surgeon was giving him scope to accept what he was most comfortable with.

Three minutes later I asked him, "What did you understand the doctor was saying to you?" In a confident voice he replied. "I've got a ninety percent chance of getting completely better and a ten percent chance of dying." He wasn't lying, his coping mechanism released to his mind and emotions all he could take at that time. In fact he lived only five months. The doctor was wise and discerning.

It would have been cruel to indicate that it was not so. We cannot torture patients by trying to force on them too much knowledge about their disease if they are not ready for it. It is best simply to answer the patient's questions and nothing more. A medical person is the person to give the medical information. Therefore, the wisest course is simply to say that you are not able to give medical details. Suggest that they write down their queries so that when a doctor comes, the direct questions may be asked.

It is amazing how many times patients will ask the question of a nonmedical person and fail to ask the doctor. In some cases, they genuinely forget to ask, being overawed by the doctor's presence. Others are frightened of learning too much, too soon.

Remember that the patient does not have to know the full details of the prognosis for the disease to run its course. The patient has "the right to know" about the illness and its implications and can insist on that right. The patient also has the "right not to know." A patient may die much happier if unaware of the full extent of the spread of the disease. Doctors should inform wise, levelheaded relatives of the full prognosis.

Reiterating the full information against the patients' wishes may mean that they fret, develop anxiety and undue fear that can mushroom, causing unbelievable stress and mental agony. One of the harmful aspects of the Kubler-Ross contribution to death education is the popularity of her five stages of dying. Medical practitioners, paramedics and the general public have become aware of her bereavement reactions. If the patient is in denial, or has not shown anger, or cried, then the social worker or some other bereavement counselor is called in by the nursing or medical personnel to talk about death. These counselors are often guilty of imposing too much too soon. They literally try to coerce the patient into premature tears or anger. The patient in crisis has needs that relate to personality and temperament and these must be considered when it comes to the speed by which the patient's perception of the condition is informed and reinforced.

Remember that every human being is unique. Reactions to physical and emotional pain differ with each of us. The pastoral person's awareness of such uniqueness should result in an effort to understand just where a particular patient is at the time of the visit.

NO NEWS GOOD NEWS?

Many People have taken comfort in the adage "No news is good news." The patient is lying in bed waiting for results of tests to determine the diagnosis or a decision on the nature of the treatment. The longer the doctors delay relaying the awaited information, the more the uncertainty and doubt fuel their fears. No news is usually perceived as bad news by patients in crisis. A common complaint is that the doctor has not told them anything, yet some of those selfsame doctors have a reputation for being open and honest with their patients.

"They know something and they are avoiding me." "They don't want to tell me." "I'm sick of being kept in the dark." The inference here, of course, is that the doctors are shielding themselves from unpleasantness by not passing on bad news.

The visitor needs to be aware of two real possibilities: firstly, the patient may have been told the situation very clearly by a doctor and had it confirmed on other occasions by the nurses, chaplain or social worker. Innumerable times the chaplain has reported such complaints only to hear from various members of staff, "I've told them the score myself." As we have already said, patients often exercise selective hearing and selective recall.

Secondly—and this is the likely cause—the doctors just don't know and cannot give a definite diagnosis. The tests are inconclusive. The patient is showing mixed, atypical symptoms and the tests are confusing. It is often difficult for the hematologist to isolate and identify the infection that is playing havoc with the treatment protocol of a leukemia patient. Medical staff usually endeavor to be honest and responsive to the patient's anxiety over "no news." Again, let it be stressed that it is not the pastoral care visitor's role to pass on medical information or criticize doctors' methods and treatment.

Sometimes the doctors are forbidden by the relatives to inform the patient, due to special circumstances which may be unknown to the pastoral person. This is an ethical issue the doctor has to come to grips with before dealing with such a patient. If the pastoral visitor is concerned over the "no news" anxiety, a word of explanation to the nursing unit manager would be proper and sufficient for any necessary action. An aggressive attitude to hospital staff for the lack of communication is not, of course, an appropriate response.

THE PROCESS OF DYING

In one generation a whole change of outlook has taken place. Hellfire and brimstone preachers are now seldom heard. People's indifference to God and the future life has grown. Scripture for the majority of people holds little influence. Although many believe in God and Jesus and still say their prayers at night, almost like wearing an amulet, theological and ontological considerations are irrelevant for great numbers of people in their day-to-day living.

When the news of terminal illness or a threat to existence comes, there is seldom a fear of "What will happen to me when I die?" or "Will I go to heaven or hell?" In many years of chaplaincy work, I have seldom been asked this by the patient. For most there is a basic fatalism: "What will be, will be." "When your number comes up you cannot do anything about it." This attitude tends to lead to the acceptance of the inevitable. Again we see in this evidence of a spiritual indifference.

There is, however, a fear of the process of dying. An accepted fallacy is that a person must always suffer prior to death, that death must be an agonizing experience. Proper medical care should relieve pain and physical distress for the terminally ill patient. Palliative care, as it currently is, aims at a comfortable, pain-free death. This means the medication is monitored and immediately adjusted to meet the pain tolerance of the patient.

Popular notions of the likely trend of the disease are often more influential than the medical staff's explanation. So, much mental torture is unnecessarily endured in anticipation of what might or might not be.

The various reactions of relatives and friends, such as overprotectiveness, apparent rejection of the patient and the disease, the decreasing regularity of visits, only escalate the patient's fear of the dying process. The message that is being received is, "It is going to be terrible to see you suffer while you are dying."

In the early stages of the disease patients with normal mental health are alert to such reactions. They are likely to interpret what they see as the visitors' abhorrence of their condition. As mentioned they often fear the worst and are looking for every indication that will confirm that fear. Illogical? Yes! But a frequent reaction.

A weekly support group for leukemia and lymphoma patients spends most of its time dealing with these fears. Long-standing patients or ex-patients in the group who share experiences are able to quell, to some extent, those terrifying, rest-disturbing thoughts.

In a paradoxical way, the sick may try to mask that fear by an apparent denial of the seriousness of the diagnosis. The brave front may hide deep internal turmoil caused by churning over possible future experiences. Thus denial appears as a coping mechanism to counter the fear of the dying process. This denial must not be mistaken for the positive attitude of the person who acknowledges the condition and is determined to beat it. Frequently, it is the person with the strong, positive attitude who responds better to treatment.

Much of the anger and violence sometimes encountered in patients is a reflection not so much of their concept of death itself but of the pain and suffering being experienced, about to be experienced, or imagined as yet to be experienced. Protestations of unfairness often relate to this anticipated process of dying. When pain is cruel, nurses in particular may be very rudely castigated. Those dedicated to the care of the terminally ill are not offended by such outbursts. They understand and expect patients to occasionally be demanding in this way.

Mr. Watson, who was very demanding, was encouraged in this attitude by an uptight family. One hectic Saturday morning when a death had

occurred in the ward, it took two of the three registered nurses on duty three hours to cope with
the persistent oozing of blood after death. The
only other registered nurse on the ward was involved with a transplant patient in isolation. Because of Mr. Watson's intolerance he was the
only patient on the ward who was given a sponge
before 1 p.m. However, in the midst of the emergency, Mr. Watson's relatives were incessantly
coming out and demanding the staff's attention.
Although Mr. Watson's condition was terminal,
he was the healthiest in the ward at that time.
The relatives reported what they perceived as the
staff's negligence to the administration. The
other more needy patients did not raise a voice,
appreciating the dilemma the staff had been in.

Mr. Watson and his relatives were behaving
inconsiderately because they knew the dying
process was going to be difficult and they hoped
by their demands it would be made easier. The
anger they demonstrated emphasized this underlying fear.

The family's demands may sometimes be a response to guilt over past bad relationships or
neglect of the patient. The visitor must be aware
of such reactions. When the likes of the Watsons
behave so selfishly, rather than getting more staff

support, they may get less—the staff may try to avoid abuse by keeping away. Good pastoral care workers have the opportunity to detect such irritating behavior and are able to provide support by trying to make positive observations about the care offered by the staff. They may tactfully point out to the relatives that their angry demands only cause greater anxiety within their loved one. This may, in fact, help ease their own tension and the patient's stress.

An unemotionally involved pastoral person can help to restore a more balanced perspective to the family. The discerning carer is able to assist the patient, relatives and staff, resulting in a more relaxed and helpful environment in the ward.

SEPARATION

When we consider terminally ill patients we should recognize the magnitude of what they are soon to experience. In most cases, excepting sudden death, of course, the patients are aware of the impending outcome of their illness. They therefore are able to reflect upon the fact that they are soon to leave everything behind. There is little they can do to alter the situation. The doctors may continue heroic efforts to prolong their lives, but deep down they know it will be of little avail. Ultimately, they will have to let go of home, assets and all their loved ones.

Lying in bed the terminally ill person has all the time to think. Particularly in the restless night hours, the mind turns to the various members of the family—father, mother, spouse, son, daughter. Where the family is loving and close, the thought of being cut off from them is like a nightmare. The fear of this separation generates more and more unrealistic hopes for their condition.

Family and other loved ones are so much the center of most of our lives. The destruction of this bond threatens the whole group. The fear is even greater when the patient is under sixty years of age; in our modern society death at such an age is considered untimely. Life has not been able to realize all its projections. Many of the pleasures associated with a growing family are not going to be witnessed and enjoyed. Who will look after this family? Although the patient may have encouraged the partner to remarry, what type of person will be the children's stepparent? This is the nagging question that remains and will remain unanswered. To imagine the children in the care of another who may have different ways and standards tortures the mind.

We often see children crying when a mother leaves them at a child care center, kindergarten or primary school for the first time. This fear in children is increased when a permanent separation is envisaged. Therefore children, whether patients or relatives, need especially attentive tender care.

Great sensitivity is required when we meet people facing such loss. The patient either allows these fears to be expressed without feeling guilty or withdraws almost to the point of refusing to speak. The hurt and aching heart needs to find release by bringing into the open those tormenting fears.

In any grieving situation, emotions rule the mind. It is often difficult and sometimes unwise to try to impose rational thinking on such a patient. A patient who is withdrawn and depressive is most likely to be absorbed with the thoughts stirred up by fears of the loss of loved ones. A gentle, supportive attitude often produces positive responses.

Any effort made to allow an opportunity for the expression of such fears will be helpful. To verbalize them aloud in front of someone else assists in bringing the situation into the right perspective. The magnitude of the event can never disappear. We must remember that and provide all the love, care, and understanding attention that we can. Only those of us who have been near death ourselves can understand something of the depth of this fear, remembering also that each person's experience is unique.

UNFINISHED BUSINESS

Most of us take life very complacently. We do what we want when we want to do it. We often go about life with the philosophy that there is plenty of time, or that tomorrow is always to be. When the doctor's pronouncement is received the truth dawns that there is not plenty of time. All the things that had been planned now may not be done. Even the things that needed to have been said, and repeated often, now no longer can be recaptivated in the same way.

A man in his early fifties had a severe heart attack. His wife had been nagging him to paint the kitchen for the previous two years but her persistence raised his stubborn streak. Now he was forbidden to get up ladders and stretch. This man worried and loaded himself with guilt because he would not be able to do the kitchen. He had let his wife down. He now also would be forced to accept the invalid pension, which meant that the hiring of tradesmen would eat into their meager savings.

An older gentleman visited his son overseas. There was a very emotional scene at the airport as they said their farewells. They both embraced, wept and told each other for the first time in about twenty years that they loved each other. A few weeks after he arrived home, the father was diagnosed with advanced lung cancer. That father wept as he realized all that he had missed out on over the years.

There are many others who do not have such an experience before they die. They cannot make amends and fear overtakes them as they begin to dwell upon what might have been, but more so on what damage and harm will continue to exist in the hearts of the survivors because they thought there would be plenty of time. Sometimes angry words are spoken that cannot be retracted. That inability to make amends arouses guilt over the incident. This may cause the terminal condition to be looked upon as a punishment, sending the patient into great fear of possible repercussions in the afterlife.

Possibly financial, emotional and relational factors are among the causes of reactions of fear in the patient: fear for the surviving relatives who may be adversely affected by the previous procrastination, plain apathy, or simple lack of planning for the future.

Such fears, created by the guilt of unfinished business, are increased when the survivors express anger at the early death of their loved one. This piling on of guilt only hastens the deterioration in the patient as the emotional torment comes into full focus. The pastoral visitor requires patience to allow these guilty fears to burst out from time to time. In fact, encouragement to voice them is necessary.

After allowing such free expression, some sense of assurance, if that is possible without blatant untruth, should be presented. Sometimes the patient is far beyond the stage of conscious recall of the past or of communication with those being left behind. Others just have never been able to express their true feelings all their lives.

The father of nine living children had not spoken to half of them for more than thirty years. Only three spent much time with him in the final stages of his illness. An apparently godless man who had lived rather selfishly all his life and seemed incapable of showing love was in a semicomatose state, not able to respond. Two daughters each held a hand while I prayed that this man might discover and experience God's peace in these final hours of earthly life. At the close of the prayer these two sisters, over forty years of age, looked at each other and with great emotion said, "He squeezed my hand." They concurred that it was the first sign of affection he had shown in their lives. They were overjoyed and tears flowed.

A few minutes later he sat up in bed, stretched out his open hands before him with a smile on his face and lay back on his pillow. He died within half an hour.

That experience of hand squeezing was spoken of at the funeral to give comfort, or rather, to ease some of the bitterness felt by most of the children toward their father. It was explained that he had the capacity to love, but was not able to show it because of some of the sad, lonely and hurtful experiences of his younger life, including four years as a Japanese prisoner of war. Seizing this flicker of light in a gloomy world of unfinishable business brought comfort.

ISOLATION

A stinging remark is often hurled by the terminally ill patient at would-be caring friends and helpers: "You don't understand how I feel." "You have never been through it, so how can you know?" In many respects the patient is right. Unless we have walked a similar path we cannot fully understand.

Now the patient will perceive, and to a large extent rightly so, that no one else has trodden that path in exactly the same way. Each patient's illness is unique. As our bodies look different, so do they react to disease and its treatment differently. I observe this daily with patients who have a terminal condition. Different people receiving the same drug protocol experience widely varying pain and other symptomatic side effects. Their response to the treatment also is widely diverse. So each individual's sickness is unique.

Each patient will experience the care and attention at home or in the hospital in different ways. The gentlest care may be deeply appreciated or received with bitter criticism. The patient's reaction to what may be termed their death sentence varies from day to day, according to the prevailing emotion or degree of pain and discomfort. Our caring ability is demonstrated by the way we adapt to the changing emotions and state of the patient. Terminally ill patients are perceptive. They are acutely aware if we really do not understand. This increases within them a sense of isolation.

Most people, when faced with the situation, are embarrassed at having to talk to a person who has been told he or she has a short time to live. In not handling this situation well, the average visitor may:

- Ignore any reference to the patient's condition, which highlights the isolation. That is, the patient's condition is a taboo subject.
- Try to deny the situation by saying that the patient looks much better. Or the very isolating remark "Go on, you are not going to die, you will live for years." Such a remark is the biggest blow to the patient's integrity you can offer.

The best way to help people who are feeling isolated is to allow them to talk about their condition, their fears, their past years. Turn on the nostalgia. Let them see that you are interested in them.

Often the staff become very close to the dying patient. Doctors as well as nurses, male and female, have wept as they have watched a long-loved terminal patient gradually slip from this world.

Isolation tears at the patient when, because of their low immune responses, they are placed in "Isolation." This means reverse barrier nursing. The restriction on visitors may stir feelings of being equated with a leper.

The specialist made a referral to the chaplain because he was concerned over the emotional instability of an HIV patient's son and his inability to cope with his mother's condition. I phoned the mother, offering to go to her home rather than have her come to the hospital. Sitting with her in her lounge room on the same lounge helped to establish the fact that I had no fear of catching AIDS. She was a normal human being and was accepted as such. That was the message she and her son received.

Similarly, when patients are in isolation we should obey isolation ward instructions but let patients see we are not scared and that our love and concern is real and genuine. If visiting is restricted, phone calls should be made to reassure them of our concern and prayers.

When a patient is swamped by feelings of isolation and ostracism, our assurances should be like casting a life belt to someone splashing in the water, struggling to be rescued.

The loneliness of isolation in any form can be eased as we show that we are prepared to willingly give up our time, convenience and even sleep to be with others. In some respects, modern medicine is cruel. It can prolong life when sometimes the quality of that life is very questionable.

Chemotherapy, radiotherapy and surgery are marvelous developments. In innumerable cases they have added years of happy life. The physician and surgeon must be guided by the success of so many patients and he or she cannot refuse to treat a patient while there is some hope of positive response to therapy. There are many cases where doctors and others have concurred that there could be virtually no chance of a reasonable life for the patient. But the prognosis has been proved wrong and the patient has recovered to go home and resume a normal life.

There are occasions, however, when these treatments with their side effects turn life into a living torture. They can stretch for a period of months or years. One patient experienced eight months like this during which he enjoyed his wife, family and home for only about three weeks. He fought on, hoping for a permanent cure. His wife regretted that he had gone through the treatment procedure.

There were times when he was more than fed up with what was going on, day in, day out, week in, week out. He lay in discomfort and agony, being relieved with painkillers. He could not support his wife. They were on an invalid pension, although he previously had his own business. He could not even do the simple things: taking his boys to soccer or the family to church. In fact, even in hospital the children exhausted him after a few minutes.

He felt that his life was utterly meaningless and painful for the family. Such thoughts bring a great amount of fear and that sense of fear stirs up a desire to die quickly rather than face a drawn-out process.

Such thoughts may in turn promote a sense of guilt. The patient interprets them as a selfishness that shows little concern for the feelings of the spouse and family that will be left behind; so guilt mounts up and adds to the fear. Frustration and impatience develop. This development leads to either irritability and lashing out at friends and loved ones or the reverse: withdrawal, depression and noncommunicativeness. The relatives become more depressed and anxious as their own sense of helplessness is magnified. All this further intensifies the feeling of isolation.

All these are logical, expected responses to the situation. Affirm that these are natural feelings. Assure that it is all right to have those thoughts; confirm that these feelings are our human part coming to the fore. Suggest that even with enforced physical inactivity and suffering, a person can still bring blessings into the lives of family and others. Love for family and loved ones needs to be received and known.

THE UNKNOWN

The allegorical picture of heaven being a city paved with gold and hell as a place of fire and brimstone, which was believed literally by so many a generation or more ago, has brought about a reaction of doubt and disbelief. The biblical literalists have done more harm than good on the average. They have brought skepticism and ridicule upon the church and its teaching, causing added confusion to the impossibility of knowing exactly what lies beyond death. This is no more evidenced than at the bedside of the average nominal Christian who is terminally ill.

This person does not really believe in anything. Is there such a place as heaven or isn't there? Increasingly people, particularly the young—those without church or Sunday school backgrounds—are accepting the position that there is nothing beyond this life. This is the finish. Among dying people, there are generally three types in my experience:

- The enthusiastic believer, who believes in a hereafter with God or Allah or whomever;
- The person who says there is nothing else, death is the end;
- The person who does not know.

It is these last two categories that hold to themselves the fear of the unknown.

An eighteen-year-old patient had been told he had less than a fortnight to live. (Actually he lived another seven days.) In conversation with him, just a few minutes after he was told the news, he said, "I'm not afraid of dying, I'm just scared because I don't know what it will be like to be nothing."

There are also those who say that they are not afraid of death but are frightened of the process of dying. What will it be like to die?

This is the fear of the unknown. It can haunt the terminally ill patient. The night hours are often spent thinking and worrying about this great unknown. Patients may be given sedation to help them sleep, so fear is suppressed until the daylight hours. To whom can they express these fears? They think people will laugh at them. Some try to get over it by saying, "God is a God of love; you don't have to worry about it." "You have led a good life—you have not been bad." This advice is cold comfort for a person with such fears.

The unknown is a frightening thing. Often patients are too sick and sedated to be involved in the kind of theological discourse designed to assure them of the fact of heaven.

The pastoral carer can, however, stress the reality of God and invite the patient to communicate with him even if it is only through prayers offered as the patient's prayer. To present the four spiritual laws for salvation or some other packaged evangelical approach would possibly be damaging. It might be rejected or produce further anxiety because the patient's condition will not permit him or her to follow logical argument.

PAIN

It is not only the terminal patient who fears the physical pain of illness. Most hospital patients experience pain to a greater or lesser degree. The ability to tolerate pain varies from person to person and often depends upon background and experience. Very insecure people will find the degree of their reaction to pain brings a corresponding degree of attention from staff. If overdone it can bring an opposite reaction as when the boy in the story called "Wolf, wolf" too often.

There are those people who create a lot of fuss over a simple intramuscular injection. Others hardly feel the prick of the needle. When a terrified patient does not see the needle and it is surreptitiously injected, it is possible that the patient may not flinch. Even if a pain is largely psychological in origin, we must accept the reality of the pain to the patient. It is real. Naturally there are those whose pain is directly proportionate to the nature of the illness, the severity of the injury, the organs or nerves affected by the condition, or the treatment being received. That pain is real. Even the most stoic show it at times. Tough, hard, "devil do-all" characters have been observed to shed tears of agony when pain from a spinal injury, for example, has electrified the body. Having once experienced such pain, the patient dreads the possibility of recurrence.

People experiencing pain are preoccupied with the pain. The caring visitor will not try to engage them in conversation unless they specifically initiate the talking. Presence is the important factor for some, while others prefer to be alone. The visitor needs to be aware of each patient's preference.

MUTILATION

Along with pain there is a fear of mutilation by the surgeon in the operating theater, or disfigurement caused by an accident, or the effects of the stroke, arthritis, muscular atrophy, burns and so on. Disfigurement affects one's public image and acceptability, in the view of the patient, who is looking at the longer-term prospects of being disabled or incapacitated. This is the fear of being less than a whole person. Mutilation may not necessarily be an outward condition. A teenage or young married person may be told that proposed chemotherapy or radiotherapy will result in the destruction of the reproductive capacities. Simply put, the patient will become sterile. This individual sees it as the destruction of part of his or her manhood or womanhood. The loss of the ability to become a parent is devastating for a young person to contemplate.

Disfigurement often brings rejection by one's peers or even spouse and children. It is noticeable how often young people will tend to stop visiting a friend who is wasting away with cancer. Older folk tend to do this too in some cases.

A mastectomy often causes a woman more anguish than any other operation. Her very body image is destroyed. She feels herself to be unattractive and unacceptable to her husband or other men. She feels herself to be less than a woman. Some women cannot bear to look at their body full-length in a mirror following such an operation. Many a husband has separated from his wife because for him some of her sexual appeal has gone. Other husbands have slept in another room and abandoned any physical intimacy with the wife. After surgery, a woman suffering such feelings of mutilation is apprehensive about leaving hospital. What will the home response be to her disfigurement?

Surgeons are aware of these responses and are continually adjusting their surgical techniques to eliminate as much disfigurement as possible. Reconstruction surgery also is amazingly successful.

Surgeons are more thoughtful these days as to where they make the incision for an operation. They try to make it in crease lines or wherever it will not affect the wearing of beach clothes.

Amputations are a most obvious form of mutilation. The loss of a foot or the leg to the knee or thigh is a horrendous thought. Many resist or delay to the last possible moment before agreeing to such surgery, much to the frustration of the surgeon. In so many cases a prosthesis, or artificial limb, can ensure that the patient resumes a more or less normal lifestyle, including some sporting activities.

In the ward there was an eighty-four-year-old evangelist of amputation. He had feared and refused the doctor's advice until he was eighty-two years old. There was then no other option: he had to have his leg amputated above the knee, or die. An artificial limb was fitted. He regained a lot of his previously lost activity. Above all he was free from pain in that limb. He came in for a second amputation when his remaining leg showed similar symptoms and because he did not want to suffer unnecessary pain, as he had done before. This eighty-four-year-old was moving around his fellow patients as an enthusiastic advocate of the success of modern artificial limbs, urging these other men and women not to hesitate having surgery.

A young man who had his wrist torn off in an industrial accident was a sporting and fitness fanatic. He saw his whole world shattered. Life wasn't going to be worth living. We talked about the possibilities of the future (as I have done with several young amputees), including a vision of participating in the disabled Olympics. The biography of Dr. Mary Verghese was given to him. This book described how she developed her reconstruction surgery skills after having both her legs smashed. She had character. At one stage in the conversation it was suggested that a whole new world was opening up to him. During a later visit his remark was exciting: "I'm better off now, I've got two worlds—this one and the one as a disabled person." He was seeing life from the two experiences. This resulted in personal growth and a positive stance toward his traumatic experience. The life-shattering became life-enriching.

Many fears of pain and mutilation are unfounded. Hospital treatment in most cases relieves pain. Mutilation and loss of parts of the body, whether internal or external, again can lead to greater personal growth and development as well as making life much more bearable physically. We can encourage these patients to acknowledge this fear, recognize its reality and then look to the positive gains physically, emotionally and for them as a person.

LOSING CONTROL

Living in a democracy the words "liberty," "civil rights," "freedom of speech" are part not only of our thinking, but of our way of life. We are taught to be independent. Schools teach our children to do their own thing, think for themselves and to make their own decisions. When hospitalized, a person comes into an institution that is regulated with a system where staff are under constant surveillance to see that hospital protocol and treatment orders are efficiently carried out. Into this environment, independent individuals are introduced as patients. Urged to obey instructions, they often are subjected to a young student nurse attending to their personal hygiene. Frequently, they are stripped of their freedom even to get out of bed. They have to do as they are told.

For a businessperson, a woman who runs her household and children, or even a child used to being able to go out to play, this produces a sense of incapacity, loss of dignity and status. For many people there is humiliation, particularly when they are not permitted to even go alone to the toilet The fear of this loss of independence and loss of control of various faculties due either to medication, surgery or an accident, raises inner anxieties that work against bodily healing. The patient's dignity and personal confidence scurry from their mind.

This fear of the loss of control is very real and patients can feel imprisoned within their own body. A young woman developed a rare disease that paralyzed her from the neck down. Even her breathing had to be assisted. She remained in hospital. She could not have existed without constant hospital supervision and facilities. Her two young children only saw her on Saturday afternoons. During the twelve months before she died, it was interesting to see her manipulation of the staff including pitting one against the other. She had to be removed from her original unit to another, the staff of the first unit forbidden to visit her. She had lost control of so much that she made efforts to control others in another way.

Patients do experience a loss of control. Patients whose condition is critical fear even greater loss of independence the longer their treatment continues. Our efforts should be to encourage them to do the things that they can. To rush to their aid and, for instance, pour them a drink that they are capable of pouring, only reinforces dependence. Any attempt to restore to them a sense of dignity and self-worth is important. "Overcare" can become overwhelming. Dignity is further eroded.

The combination of uncertainties, confusions, fears, anxieties, information and misinformation, fact and suppositions is never the same in any two patients, nor is it the same on any two visits. Effective pastoral visitation in hospital depends upon the minister, priest or lay visitor being fully aware of this. It requires time to sense where the patient is. It must be remembered that the patient is often acting out of character due to the illness. Perhaps, for example, the church-going religious facade is not providing the same camouflage that is maintained outside the hospital. This revelation may be startling for the visitor.

The necessity to try and understand the complexity of feelings highlighted in this chapter cannot be overstressed. Begin your visit by assessing these. A similar time for assessment must be taken each visit and issues half concluded in the previous visit should not be taken up until the appropriateness is ascertained. It may not be relevant on this visit.

Simply put, good advice is "Get to know your patient's state of body, mind and spirit first on each visit." This leads to good pastoral care.

NOTES

1. Elisabeth Kubler-Ross, *On Death and Dying: What the Dying Have to Teach Doctors, Nurses, Clergy, and Their Own Families*, 34–121.

2. Stated by Kubler-Ross at a workshop in Sydney 1979.

→ CHAPTER 3 ←

Temptations

There are a number of eager people who seek opportunities to visit hospitals as a form of Christian
service. Frequently such people come up and say
to me "I love hospital visitation. You are able to
get alongside really needy people." To love hospital visitation is an inappropriate expression. Hospital visitation is exacting: it demands concentration and so often is physically, spiritually and
emotionally draining. Often it can appear unre-
warding. Such times are compensated for by those
very fulfilling, positive, even if vitality-sapping,
traumatic ministrations to distraught, frightened,
angry or hurting patients or relatives. There are
also those visits to some of God's saints, who minister more to you than you do to them.

The reception of the offered cup of water in
Christ's name is often treated with suspicion and

even sometimes scorn, but others will drink and Christ is honored.

To hear a person say that she or he loves hospital visitation is to hear warning bells concerning that person's effectiveness around the wards. Most experienced, trained workers, as well as hospital pastoral workers new to visitation, all face temptations when they come to the bedside or are dealing with relatives. Some of the more common temptations covered here may find earlier echoes in this book. They are reintroduced here in another guise to reinforce an awareness of our need to be conscious of the pitfalls. All of us face them, all of us will continue to succumb to them on occasions.

TO SET A PROGRAM

Is this a familiar scenario? A hospital visit is planned. The pocket edition of the New Testament and Psalms is taken, after carefully selecting the passage that will be read. The same reading is used for each patient. Of course the traditional passages are trotted out. One day a partly deaf lady at a nursing home loudly explodes, "Why is it that you ministers always read Psalm 103?" The lesson is learnt!

If a visitor goes along with a set program for four patients—allowing twenty minutes each—subconsciously there is recorded that after about fifteen minutes there must be the Bible reading and prayer before leaving. The offer of these is the indication that the visit has ended.

Such set programs take no account of the circumstances of each patient. It can be safely assumed that the same passage of Scripture will *not* meet the needs of all four patients. They will be in differing stages of hospitalization. Their needs, physical and spiritual, will require different touches.

A set program or agenda will not provide an effective ministry. One chaplain, who developed a set routine, boasted of visiting over a hundred patients each day. His ministry was considered worthless by patients and staff of the hospital. The staff would call others in an emergency rather than send for him.

Those who set agendas are more preoccupied with self-achievement than the welfare of the patient or family. Self-achievement as a goal can be a threat to hospital ministry.

PAUSES IN CONVERSATION

Whether it be in a prayer meeting or at a hospital bedside, it is surprising how we are embarrassed by silence. There are many situations when silence is so necessary for the patient. The patient may be unable to concentrate through debilitation, tiredness, drug effects, or sheer pain and discomfort. Your silent presence on such occasions is the most appropriate form of care needed.

A patient may be so bewildered and confused that a multiplicity of thoughts are rivaling each other for the mind's attention. Your chatter may add further distraction to an already-overcrowded mind.

Your presence or something you said may have raised issues about which there is a desire for discussion. The patient, recognizing the need to open up, is also reticent to make the disclosure. The struggle to find the opening gambit is disturbed if the pastoral visitor's uncomfortableness with the silence is obvious.

Pauses in conversations may indicate many things. They often provide the opportunity to regroup thoughts or to allow what has just been said to be fully applied and digested. Rushing in to break the silence may squash and repress the very thing that might have made the visit productive.

TO BECOME THE FOCUS

A minister or an official pastoral visitor has a special status and position. There is a certain expectation by the patient that the visitor often feels must be seen to be fulfilled. His or her job seems to be to make sure that conversation flows. To keep the conversation going it is easy to talk about personal experiences. The whole meeting then becomes centered on the visitor. The patient's needs and circumstances are fully put aside. It becomes a lively, happy, interesting and perhaps even informative time. The visitor becomes the star, the patient the ignored.

Visitors sometimes delight in talking about their own periods of hospitalization and their own close encounters with death. It is an almost irresistible topic. At other times the visitor's illnesses become the depressing focus of the visit, which is even more disastrous.

The visitor probably departs feeling elated that everyone was responsive. Prayer was offered. The visit was successful. The patient when alone might think it was nice of the visitor to call—but! He or she may also smart at the slight shown during the visit.

So obsessed was the visitor with making the visit a success that the real reason for it was lost in the parade of self. When self comes to the fore, the wrong motivation becomes evident

TO "OUTTALK" THE PATIENT

A variation on the temptation for the carer to do most of the talking is the person who is a compulsive talker. This type of person is a chronic interrupter of conversation, who "talks over" other people. Such persons have real difficulties with truly listening to others. Very often they volunteer for a hospital visitation role, where they find a captive audience with little reserve or energy to put them in their place.

They are often kindly people who have an open heart. They are eager to help but their need to be accepted is greater. It is generally recognized that this need to talk, to help and to be accepted has its origins in unsatisfactory childhood relations.

This type of person should be recognized when a lay pastoral team is being selected. It is not easy to cull such people from a hospital visitation program without hurting the already-sensitive feelings that are the cause of their compulsive talking.

Patients may become deeply distressed and anxious when they are not being heard because a visitor is talking over them all the time. The priest or minister or lay pastoral team leader should be ever conscious of the possibility of such a person being in the group. This is where supervision and feedback from the group is so important in hospital ministry.

TO COMPARE PATIENTS

At times, chaplains as well as other pastoral visitors find themselves guilty of likening the patient's condition to that of similar and even dissimilar cases. Some visitors have a penchant for describing every like diagnosis they have experienced or heard about. The odd illustration of a case may be made to help a patient deal with a particular situation, to encourage hope. Sometimes it may be necessary by this means to prepare the patient for the reactions that may be expected from the treatment. A comparison may be the balm to soothe unrealistic fears.

The danger in citing other cases is that firstly you do not have the full medical facts of both cases to justify making comparisons. Secondly, the other case may be that of an identifiable person. It is unethical to use the case without that person's permission. Thirdly, it is likely that your reference to anybody else indicates to the patient, immersed in his or her own situation, that you are not really interested in him or her. Fourthly, you are likely to be judged as one interested only in airing your knowledge.

TO PROVIDE SOLUTIONS

One of the most abused terms today is the word "counselor." It seems that anyone who completes some short course or attends a number of seminars or conferences feels justified in calling her or himself a counselor. We hear of telephone counselors, bereavement counselors, family counselors and so on. Unless they have done several hundreds of hours of supervised counseling they have no right to be called counselors. Lay pastoral care courses and even most theological college courses do not entitle a minister or a visitor to be classified as a counselor.

Many bedside encounters see the visitor coming in as the counselor like a ferret trying to find a problem or difficulty needing solution. Some pastoral care workers feel as if their visit has not been successful unless they have been able to be the knight in shining armor riding to the rescue of the patient.

Pastoral visitors have no brief to prove that they are counselors extraordinaire. The attempt may satisfy the ego needs of the carer (placing a question mark on the title "carer" in such circumstances), but does little for the confidence of the patient. The perceptive patient recognizes that the visit is most probably to fulfill those needs. There are the occasions when patients are seeking some comfort, help and advice. More likely the need is to sort matters out themselves with a little guidance. The carer becomes the facilitator for the patient to begin to view events less subjectively. The patient is given room to think out aloud, to reappraise and to change mental, emotional and spiritual attitudes.

Mrs. Jones had just been told of the need to have urgent surgery. Her disease was life-threatening and she was told that surgery might give her two or three more years. She didn't want her children upset by the news. The doctor had left her to talk it over with the family and let him know the decision the next day. I was called to Mrs. Jones because she was very depressed and feared surgery. She pleaded with me to tell her what to do. This was my first visit. After having the above scenario outlined to me prior to the visit I said, "Well, let's look at the situation."

I got her to talk about her children and her grandchildren, the nature of their relationship, what their hopes and aspirations were. Mrs. Jones also outlined what she wanted to do and looked at the possibilities.

What had the doctor said, I asked. She reported that the doctor had said if her heart stood up to the surgery and she came through, there was every chance of no further trouble although he would commit himself to no more than two or three years. Prior to my seeing Mrs. Jones, I had ascertained that the prognosis following surgery was reasonably good.

Mrs. Jones shared her feelings about an early death. She also became excited about what it would mean if the operation were successful. Without expressing my own mind, I continued to let her talk until she came to the decision to go ahead with the surgery. It was worth the risk, she decided.

We prayed for a right attitude of mind and spirit by Mrs. Jones as she went to theater, as well as for her to experience God's guidance through the surgery and after. She told the family of her decision that evening.

Mrs. Jones came through the surgery successfully, having entered theater with a deep peace, which came from her feeling of having made the right decision.

It was her decision, she was not coerced into it. This fact was possibly a significant factor in the success of the surgery. The chaplain facilitated the decision but did not make it for her.

TO ORGANIZE THE PATIENT

Enfeebled by illness, the patient often presents a picture of helplessness and forlornness. The pastoral carer in an image of health and vitality, might come marching in, mistakenly thinking to produce in the patient a better state of mind, a smile on the face, a happier and a more peaceful disposition.

Helplessness may stimulate maternal or paternal instincts in the carer. The need to smother the patient with overconcern becomes a distinct possibility. The patient begins to visualize the carer as a type of old-fashioned matron, who busily fluffs up the pillow, fills the water jug with fresh water, redoes the floral arrangement, tidies up the bedside locker, reads the get well cards, asks who they are from and orders tea or even holds the cup or props up the head to enable the patient to drink the afternoon tea.

The visitor is thus in control, organizing the patient—yes, and even at times ringing for the staff to do this or that for the patient. This looks very good to the visitor. The feeling of doing something worthwhile is exhilarating. The visitor is on a high.

The patient, however, may not be up to being fussed over. Rather than appreciating this fuss, he or she may resent it. The dominating visitor may seem to be tightening the screws of helplessness. The spirit of the patient may be crushed even further. A domineering pastoral visitor wearies and saps away a little more of the patients' dwindling physical reserves. Encouraging patients, instead, to do something for themselves is often more helpful.

TAKE OVER THE ROLE OF THE RELATIVES

A pastoral visitor may not be an overpowering person, but driven by the demand to be a good pastoral worker, she or he may feel a strong desire to become an indispensable figure to the patient. Seeing to a number of things is the prerogative of relatives or other closer friends. These include washing the patient's clothes, mowing the patient's lawn and watering the garden, paying accounts (such as telephone and electricity) that cannot be deferred. The offer to pay such accounts, like many other manipulative approaches of this nature, may become more than offers. The patient may feel obligated to give permission to proceed to do these tasks.

This type of role assumption and the need to feel indispensable may not only cause distress to the patient but also lead to friction between the relatives and the patient. The pastoral worker must defer to the relatives' position.

Hospitalization of a sick relative provides the opportunity for some relatives to make up for previous neglect and lack of communication and concern. Such relatives are resentful of a visitor who appears to usurp their role. That antagonism increases if they are thwarted from assuaging their guilt for those years of disinterest by not being able to make these practical efforts now for the ease and comfort of the patient's mind.

Where patients have no interested relations or friends, such help may be very appropriate and appreciated. Other members of the church family may be involved to further encourage these patients, showing that people are interested in them and care for them. If you are a busy pastoral person, then other people with practical skills and time should be given the opportunity to exercise them.

TO FORCE LOGICAL AND RATIONAL POSITIONS

We have already noted that one of the coping mechanisms of patients facing a difficult prognosis is to hear only as much as they are able to bear at the time. It is extremely difficult to listen to a patient talking about resuming athletics training when you know of mutilated tendons and calf muscles. This particular patient had been on his way to the top. The Commonwealth and Olympic games had seemed a real possibility. Now there was no way that track events could feature in his future.

"How kind it would be to snap him back to reality." "We can't let him keep going on with this delusion." "He must begin to face reality and try to think positively about life without athletics." These thoughts entered a lot of John's visitors' minds. The fact is that John had been told about his condition by the doctors and it had been confirmed by nurses and physiotherapists. John at that stage was unable to grapple with the thought of a life without physical prowess. The blow of the accident also affected study and employment prospects.

Impatience on the part of the pastoral care visitor can rival family pressure to be the one to put the patient right. The pressure to force John to accept a logical and rational appraisal of his position was hard to resist. What I did was encourage him to maintain hope for a fulfilling and satisfying future life. I spoke of standing for the club's committee and of the opportunities available in his less physical activities.

There may come an appropriate time to reinforce the true situation. However, it would have been unwise to lock into John's subconscious the conviction that he would never again be useful. That would be a very depressing prospect for a virile youth to tackle. His denial of this gives him something to fight to regain self-acceptance.

Much response to hospital and other treatment is due to a positive mental approach. To destroy that approach by coercing a patient to accept reality prematurely is likely to impair the will to recover. It is likely to be presumptuous on the part of the pastoral care worker to assume the responsibility to press the issue. Where it develops, after a long period, into a pathological issue, then more professional help may need to be sought.

This applies to all hospital cases where a radical lifestyle change appears the only option or where there is a terminal diagnosis.

As a postscript, since writing the above, I have received news that John has won gold at a World Disabled Games in Japan, in the discus event, using arm and shoulder muscles rather than damaging his legs.

TO TAKE UP THE CUDGELS

The patient and the family sometimes are overwhelmed with the magnitude of their impending loss and the current circumstances. They are all in a state of shock. They feel they must be seen to be doing something for the patient. This is particularly true when the patient has always been mollycoddled by the family. Equally so, at the other extreme—when previously the patient has been neglected—the need to assuage the guilt of that indifference is keenly felt.

In such cases, the patient in the relatives' eyes becomes the only and most important patient there ever was. Service is expected beyond a consideration of staff responsibility to other patients. When that is not forthcoming, the staff are castigated for presumed inefficiencies, such as the noon medicine rounds not coming till 12:15 p.m. or a nurse taking ten minutes to answer the call bell.

It is the basic assumption that the person from the church should carry more weight than relatives. The pastoral visitor is drafted into taking up the cudgels on behalf of the patient The family often accompany the carer to see that he or she says and does what they have tutored him or her to say and do! The staff, however, are likely to treat the church visitor as one being manipulated by the family and so take little notice.

It is easy to be overwhelmed, like the relatives, at the loss being envisaged. The pastoral carer, through closeness to the family, may lose objectivity and become the defender and champion of the patient. Yet not always are the relatives' assumptions correct. Doctors' communications are not always interpreted accurately. The patient's and relatives' expectations of what should be done or what can be happening may be unrealistic given the nature of the case.

If you are tempted to take up the cudgels on behalf of the patient or family, it is wise to go alone to the hospital staff, and ask quietly about what is happening. It may be diplomatic to say you think there may be some misunderstanding and you would like to clear it up with the family. Such an approach will often bring cooperative responses and give you a much different picture. The staff may then seek your cooperation in helping the relatives to understand. The warning is: Be sure of your facts before you become the champion of an alleged underdog.

TO DISSEMINATE KNOWLEDGE

Hospitals are involved with the lives of people. From the hospital's side all barriers are down. The patient's privacy in many areas no longer exists. The staff know the condition and often the cause of the condition. In some cases, such as sexually transmitted diseases, for example, it is a very personal affair. A person's bodily ills are their own personal matter yet they become necessary knowledge for the hospital and all too often this knowledge becomes available to the church, too. The church bulletin can become a serious offender in this regard.

Unfortunately, the source of information for those newssheets is sometimes the pastoral visitor. Yet to pass on such information without the permission of the patient and the relatives is a breach of confidentiality and is therefore indictable. A vindictive person could take you to court. These days the laws are very strict.

Requests have come from some patients who are active in their churches not to inform their parish minister of their stay in hospital. The reason is basically that they do not want the nature of their illness broadcast. It is sad that people have to forego spiritual comfort and help because pastoral people breach confidentiality sometimes.

Be worthy of the confidence placed in you during your hospital visitation.

TO ASSUME THE SOLE PASTORAL ROLE

As an official visitor—priest, minister, sister, brother, deaconess or other religious leader—you are the one recognized by the church to offer pastoral care to a particular patient or family. You may not be the only pastoral person to call upon the patient regularly. Others may be a personal family friend of long standing or a Christian work colleague who has shared many confidences over a long association. It may be a minister who married the patient or shared earlier life dramas. It may be the acquaintance who introduced the patient to the church scene. The person may be a trained person or an ordinary church member with no great claim to previous pastoral ministry.

Where pastoral care has become an ego-dominated ministry; where pride in being able to get on with people is projected; where there is a feeling of being better than others at visitation; and where personal status is important, then the temptation to adopt the role of sole pastoral carer becomes strong.

The patient or the relatives may have a greater rapport with another pastoral worker. It then becomes an embarrassment, confusing and disturbing for the patient, if the official church visitor subtly takes over. The patient and family may be hurt. The preferred visitor feels frustrated and angry, being thwarted in his or her efforts to provide the pastoral care the patient desires and needs. Competition in these circumstances is destructive for the patient, visitors and carers.

The grace to recognize and to defer to another, more appropriate person is a demonstration of your fitness to be involved in pastoral care. An inflated sense of ego is not needed in the hospital scene.

TO EXPECT A PATIENT'S OUTPOURINGS

Sometimes professional healthcare workers are referred to a patient whom nursing staff may consider to be acting inappropriately under the circumstances. They see the patient. They probe and delve until they get the emotional or other results they expect. Such tactics are often resented strongly by the patient and family.

Similarly, pastoral care workers can fall into the trap of considering that unless the patient has revealed something of their inner selves and feelings, the visit has been of little value. Such role expectation falls far short of what pastoral care is. It may take weeks, even months, before any free sharing may be possible. It may be that personal sharing of deeper feelings never occurs. This does not mean that the previous pastoral visits have been failures.

Patients may have no need to bare feelings

and emotions. They are coping and have the very strong supportive care of family and friends. They may be having considerable drug treatment or recovering from an operation and finding it a struggle to concentrate on anything. To be forced to try and stir up even dormant feelings is just too much effort. It may be completely unnecessary. It is an intrusion of privacy in such cases.

A pastoral care worker who considers that care is not being given unless a "deep and meaningful" conversation has eventuated is putting role expectations above the best interests of the patient. A patient is under no obligation to accept the pastoral care visitor or to reveal more than he or she wishes.

TO CONCENTRATE ON SOMETHING ELSE

There are two aspects of this temptation that need to be understood. The first is patient-initiated. Patients may not desire to be involved in any discussion about themselves or their illness with you as a church representative. This is their right. In exercising this prerogative they may deliberately turn the conversation to every other topic to occupy the time and save embarrassment. Attention is often deliberately directed to another patient for this reason.

To understand the real reasons for these diversionary tactics you should be alert. Possibly it is an indication that the patient is avoiding any serious involvement with the church. Or there may be something about you that is providing a barrier to confidence. An earlier unpleasant experience with the church may contain the embers of resentment and possible bitterness. Again, the patient may be still denying the seriousness of the illness and would not be able to cope with reality at this stage. Another possibility is that the patient is harboring some guilt feeling toward the church and you have become a reminder of the spiritual ulcer within.

The second aspect is the initiation of the diversion by the pastoral visitor, who finds it difficult to come to grips with the patient's condition. Rather than face the uncomfortableness of talking about the illness and concentrating on the patient, the carer sees other subjects as safer. However, although the conversation might be interesting, informative and even spiritually uplifting, when the patient is struggling with his or her own doubts, anger and grief, such otherwise grippingly important themes fall flat. And the patient is patently aware of the large detour the carer is taking.

Again the pastoral visitor must be aware of what is happening within the patient. A helpful line when the sidetracking is being done by the patient is to accept it. Other times it should be noted that the guilt or fear being experienced is what the patient is desirous of facing, yet hesitant personally to open out on the subject. Perceptive skills, adeptness at gently lifting lids, and empathy make the combination needed. The pendulum must swing.

TO STAY TOO LONG

Sometimes there is a tendency to stay too long. The patient may be the only one you have to visit in the hospital. The thought arises, "I've taken the trouble to come, so I may as well make it worthwhile." Depending upon the illness, the stage of its development, and the condition of the patient, a long visit may be the last straw. Your visit may become a further endurance trial for the patient.

On the other hand, your presence for a long period silently sitting there while the patient dozes, may be just the comforting assurance needed to relax enough to get some of that elusive sleep. Time and again as a chaplain I have found it possible to support a patient until she or he has fallen into a deep sleep and the grip on my hand has loosened, allowing it to be slipped out. The next call may then be made. Time spent like this is of immense value to the patient. For this to happen the patient must feel comfortable in your presence and be given full permission to sleep without any offense. The length of stay is assessed by your own sensitivity to the patient's needs.

There are pastoral workers who have assumed that the object of their visit is to cheer up the patient. There is a seemingly subconscious acceptance of the entertainer's role. It is viewed as a time of filling in the lonely hours for a patient. A pastoral visitor's role in a general hospital is not that. There may be some very lonely or frightened patients who may need and appreciate your presence, but not as an entertainer. Rather they would prefer you as an understanding friend who is able to listen to them without being advice-giver or counselor and who is able to appreciate true companionship at such a time. The entertainer seldom realizes when enough is enough. A showman is rarely welcomed by a very sick person.

Another reason for a prolonged stay may be that the visitor is waiting for an opportunity to say goodbye. Other visitors are monopolizing the conversation—you are sitting back and listening. It would appear rude to interrupt. In such cases your visit is not very productive. Your time might be more profitably spent with someone else. Politely excuse yourself, unless the patient requests you to stay in the hope that the other talkative people will depart instead.

Sometimes a carer might find it hard to conclude a visit because of a sense of not having accomplished what was intended. The agenda-setting fallacy is producing guilt feelings. Consider that a visit committed through prayer to the Holy Spirit's guidance *has that guidance*. Your own agenda may be most inappropriate at that time. Accept the situation. To prolong the visit waiting for your opportunity to do your thing may be closing those doors of opportunity to you forever.

Let it be repeated, sensitivity is the key in determining the length of time spent at each bedside.

TO BE THE EVANGELIST

There are those, both clergy and laity, who believe Christians must present the gospel or be assured that the patient is right with the Lord every
time they visit a bedside. If the patient should die
that night, they would feel responsible for his or
her eternal status, good or bad, the latter being
the greater.

There are some very basic theological and ethical flaws in this attitude. Without the Holy Spirit
being able to break through and prepare a person's spirit for any sort of spiritual impact in his
or her life, all our talking is of little consequence.
If the Holy Spirit does the work, we must be working in partnership and cooperation with that same
Holy Spirit. Not every person is ripe for the har-
vest. In normal experience the Spirit would not
give carte blanche to any individual to approach
any and every patient this way. Every patient is
not ready for, or in a fit state to comprehend the
message of the gospel. Experience proves that
with many the attempt to preach it drives an even
bigger wedge between the person and the church,
God and the carer. It also can cause a sudden deterioration in the patient's condition.

Any approach to the patient in this way should be with the patient's permission and when the patient is not too distressed with the progress of the disease. Partnership with the Spirit will enable the carer to detect the right moment—if there is to be one—when the Spirit wishes to use him or her for such an encounter.

A rigid and fixed agenda is likely to be cold, clinical and mechanical. It is similar to the door knocking routine of certain religious enthusiasts. The acutely perceptive patient is apt to switch off, hearing little of what is being communicated. Elsewhere it has been pointed out that God is able to use many avenues and resources beyond the theological method we cling to so dearly.

The visitor has to earn the right from the patient to raise spiritual matters. It is seldom in a first visit that sufficient rapport is built up to launch into selling the gospel. Even if the patient was previously known to the visitor, circumstances have changed. The cause of hospitalization may be concealing many matters unknown to the visitor. To assume a right to know under such circumstances may be counter-productive. Time is required to ascertain if that is possible, where the patient is spiritually. Probing into the personal may be a breach of privacy.

Similarly, uninvited spiritual delving is breaching privacy. If your visit has been committed to God's guidance, allow the Spirit to open the door for you. A forced entry is unappreciated.

There is so much that we have to learn about God; we should not place limitations and expect God to conform to our ideas. Hospital visitation requires a great trust. We must believe, along with Job, that our just God will do what is right.

TO BE UNNATURAL

A hospital is an unnatural environment. People tend to act unnaturally there. The patient is treated unnaturally by relatives and visitors. For most people, medicine carries the feeling of the mystical. The doctors' language is often hard to decode. The nurses are rushing, busy, busy, busy. Pastoral carers likewise tend to approach the bedside differently from the way they handle other situations. There must of course be a difference because of the circumstances, but that difference should not interfere with your being yourself with the patient.

An artificial voice, whispered tones, nervous body language, stilted conversation, taboo subjects, wary responses, or exuberant laughter and loud talk are signs of the unnatural. It is all part of a game: the "Conspiracy Play," the "Near Death Drama," the "Panic Opera" or perhaps the "Marilyn Melodrama." There are times when the pastoral worker gets sucked into this unnaturalness.

Basically the patient requires you to act naturally when all else around is seemingly unnatural. There are certain normal restraints required in hospital visitation. To go beyond that is to indicate the unnatural.

In being yourself, you are being true to yourself and honest with the patient. In the midst of the artificiality around, the patient will be more likely to respond to you if you are yourself, and your ministry will, therefore, be more acceptable.

TO COERCE THE PATIENT

In any ministry we expect results. Hospital ministry can bring with it an air of urgency. The patient may or may not survive. The shortage of time can put pressures upon the pastoral person to try to get the patient to complete as much unfinished business as possible. Perhaps some relationships are strained.

Suppose the patient and another person in the church have had a running feud over the years. It is desired that they accede to some form of reconciliation. The obstinacy still continues in spite of the threat to the life of the hospitalized parishioner.

With all good intentions, the pastoral carer sets out to find a solution. The temptation is to manipulate the patient to admit wrong attitudes, to express regret over what has happened, to seek reconciliation. This is all in order that the patient might die in peace. In one way or another the visitor tries to force words out of the patient, words which the patient does not want to say. Or, even more unethical, to offer a prayer on behalf of the patient using the words the patient refuses to utter. (Confrontation is considered in chapter 5.)

To coerce the patient into speaking or to say the words for him or her, implies that the patient is forced into a position or meaning which the visitor desires him or her to adopt and not what may be best.

The manipulative deceit of this type of move generally causes adverse reaction and hostility within the patient. At other times, being so debilitated and not wishing to get further agitated, the patient acquiesces to the visitor's maneuvers but unwillingly. The whole exercise is a falsehood.

The patient often gives in just to get the visitor to depart more quickly. The zealous evangelist is prone to succumb to this temptation.

Manipulation is a temptation to which zealous evangelists are particularly prone. Coercion of a dying patient or critically ill person is morally and ethically wrong and cannot be accepted as Christian behavior.

TO HIDE BEHIND THE SCRIPTURES

The hospital is the place to hear questions and doubts about God that are unanswerable. Challenges to faith are seriously made. Even the most devout find it difficult to accept the unfairness of some of the pain and suffering experienced. Job-like situations are faced.

Many pastoral care workers, including theologically trained clergy, find answers that are logically integrated hard to come by. It is difficult to discover responses that satisfy theologically acceptable norms. Theology and practice seem poles apart.

It is tempting to produce a copy of Scriptures and read some of the promises therein. The patient is told that God's grace is sufficient. The words of Christ, promising never to leave or forsake us, are expected to provide comfort. Psalms urging "trust in the Lord with all your might" stir skepticism. The Scriptures are offered as a blanket cover to challenges to faith, and to question them is considered a sin. The guilt associated with doubt is added to the heavy burden already imposed upon the patient.

Some pastoral care workers hide behind Scriptures as a ruse to avoid the unanswerable embarrassments. The patient, however, requires direct personal communication. To read Scriptures in such circumstances seldom is effective. In my view it more often destroys communication. If Scriptures are to be used, they should not destroy the eyeball-to-eyeball communion. Scriptures should flow sincerely from the heart, out of your own experience. The Scripture should be made vital and alive, not at odds with the current ordeal the patient is experiencing. The printed page kept in the pocket, while its truth, relevant to the practical needs of the patient, flows out of the mouth, is the ideal. Where this is not possible, it is best to reserve the scripture for a more acceptable occasion, if it arises. WHERE THERE IS DOUBT AND READY ANSWERS ARE NOT FORTHCOMING, BE HONEST, ADMIT YOU DON'T HAVE AN ANSWER.

There are other temptations facing the hospital visitor. Chaplains, visiting clergy and lay pastoral workers all, in varying degrees of frequency, fall into these snares. Combining training, experience, empathy, awareness and sensitivity will reduce the rate and regularity of the falls.

True pastoral care is hard and demanding work. We can take heart from the knowledge that the Holy Spirit has promised to give wisdom and understanding for each circumstance.

→ CHAPTER 4 ←

The Place of Prayer

An innate trait of the human race is the ability to pray. For many it has been suppressed by social pressures, scientific skepticism or the current growth of humanism, which sees God as of little or no relevance to human existence. "Immortalists," a relatively new philosophical group, are waiting for medical science to advance to the point where humans will not die. They want to live on earth forever without aging and firmly believe that in the next generation this will be quite possible. It will make God and the need for prayer irrelevant, they say.

Yet, in spite of religious apathy, agnosticism, or antagonism, that inherent tendency to pray in a crisis remains. Across the millennia there have been those who have been set apart to communicate with the deity or deities on behalf of other people. All religions have had their shamans, priests and ministers to intercede for others.

Since the advent of Christ, the individual's right to pray directly to God has become a distinctive feature of Christianity. With education and the general liberation of access to theological knowledge and experience in Christianity, prayer individually, in small groups and corporately, has become more generally practiced. In hospital, the patient is often longing to hear a prayer offered to God on his or her behalf.

In their pastoral duties in hospitals fewer chaplains are using manuals in their visitations. Lay pastoral workers are increasingly using prayer as a means of bringing spiritual assurance, comfort and hope at the bedside. Personal prayer becomes for many the focal point of the pastoral visit.

The two big questions that we will deal with in this chapter are: when and how to pray?

WHEN TO PRAY

Prayer "is a most powerful tool and requires care in its use." These are potent words from Richmond,1 who warns that it is possible to abuse prayer. It is sometimes used as a weapon, by busy people, to get away from the talkative patient. Others may use it as a means of avoiding issues the patient is raising.

Two traditional concepts

There are two traditional concepts as to when a visitor on a pastoral call should pray:

- on every visit
- only when asked

1. Praying on every visit

Whether a home or hospital visitation, it was always expected that a priest or pastor should pray with the person or family on every visit. This has become a tradition. Some lay pastoral care courses even promote it. Thus there are those pastoral workers who have ticked it off as a regular "to do" of pastoral visitation.

Not only is there a sense of expectation that a hospital visit must include prayer, but pastoral visitors may use prayer to maintain a role, to project an image. In such cases whether the patient desires it or would like to reject it, prayer becomes the essential ingredient for the successful visit. We should ask, "Whose need is being met?"

There are dangers in making prayer a fixed rule for every visit:

Ritualization. Prayer becomes ritualized when it is part of the agenda for every visit. The tendency is to carry a prayer book or one of the minister's manuals that has prayers for the visitation of the sick. If these are said by rote, almost without reading the words, they come across to the patient as lacking in sincerity and real interest in the patient. The visitor is just fulfilling the role expected.

A chaplain was showing me over his hospital at 10:30 A.M., time for his daily administration of the Eucharist. He had his denominational list for the ward with him. He went to each bed, moving from one patient to the next within three minutes, not inquiring if anyone desired the Eucharist—he did not even ask about the patients' health. I was left wondering as to the helpfulness of a ritual with such little personal application. There was virtually no conversation between chaplain and patient—just the reading from the manual and the offering of the host.

Even the administration of other sacraments, such as the anointing of the sick, may be interpreted in a similar vein. Prayer and the sacraments must contain more personal meaning for the patient than the mere fulfilling of a ritual obligation.

The inclusion of the patient's name does not of itself indicate a personal concern by the carer.

Generalization. When prayer is expected to be offered at every bedside it is possible to detect a pattern in each prayer and visit. The prayers become generalized: a bit of theology; thanksgiving for the hospital staff, for the patient's healing, even when the prognosis is poor; and finally a prayer for the patient's family (usually vague on details). It more or less is a prayer where God is asked to bless them all—whatever that would mean to a patient feeling particularly unblessed! The sigh of the patient on seeing the visitor enter muffles an inaudible "not again" or "for goodness sake, go away." Such feelings about the pastoral visitor are sometimes relayed to the fulltime chaplain or other staff members.

Superficiality. A ritual or general prayer may also be perceived as being superficial and shallow. Visitors who always pray are either very confident of their ability as pastoral care workers or, at the other extreme, are very nervous and do not know what to say. The confident ones breeze in as if in control and offer prayer without much thought, because they have done it so many times before. Let the reminder be sounded again—patients are very perceptive of superficiality.

The nervous person, on the other hand, usually prays in the familiar language of the church, to cover up the awkwardness of inexperience, embarrassment or even a fear of identification with the patient. This results in an inability to become involved. The relationship and the prayer remain at a superficial level. The patient feels little comfort from such a visit which may in fact, stir up anger.

Piety. Even the most conscientious visitor steeped in his or her religion is often bound by theological upbringing from early childhood. Language has changed. The younger generation is more realistic about life and religion. If the old pious talk at the bedside is repeated in the prayer, a sentimentalism is detected that in no way suits the patient's condition. Even active churchgoers are sometimes irritated by such pietistic praying. Much of the meaning and intent is garbled because of the mix of religious language. The patient may begin to wonder whether the visitor knows what the prayer really means.

Self-righteousness. The role of a pastoral care person in a hospital should carry with it a sense of responsibility. Very often visitors have little training and experience. Sometimes they interpret experiences wrongly and, like little Jack Horner, say "What a good boy am I!" In fact he was a naughty boy for putting his thumb in the pie. These people have an underlying feeling that they have to prove to the patient and the church they are competent for the task of pastoral care. Their prayers they see as a means of advertising that they are spiritually right. The prayers are flowery, showing their wide range of scriptural knowledge and reverence of God. They are avenues for the display of self-righteousness. Of course the report goes back to the church of how well accepted they were and how their prayer was very much appreciated. Whether this really was the case or not is beside the point. The appearance of being sincere and faithful in ministry was maintained.

Authoritarianism. There is a tendency to accept that if a certain act, procedure or ritual is performed, the one officiating has a function elevated above the others. An inner tension is often there until the task has been performed. The officiator perhaps is aware of this and assumes command until the duty is complete. The need to orchestrate procedures and the timing of them is a matter of prestige. Frequently that pressure rises until the order comes, "Let us Pray," or, in a more patronizing way, "Would you mind if I prayed with you?" The latter really gives no option for the patient who, feeling like a captive, is obliged to keep this authority figure from the church happy.

The patient is in an inescapable trap. The prayer that follows is often accompanied by seething inner feelings at this further whittling away of the patient's independence and dignity. This, of course, goes completely unnoticed by the carer who has apparently fulfilled his or her appointed responsibility.

Even a polite "May I have prayer with you?" puts patients on the spot. To refuse outright leaves them open to the judgment of being unspiritual. What Perry and Sell wrote of the depressed patient may be equally said of many other kinds of patients we visit: *"Sometimes when you feel down, you don't need more prayer . . . You need a good night's sleep. . . .* When there is adequate cause for feelings of depression we should not feel an urgent need to get right with God or to restore the joy of salvation."2

Heretical as this may sound to people of the "always pray" tradition, it carries much sound Christian counseling wisdom. People need to work through some of their bitterness and anger—perhaps even toward God—at being hospitalized, before prayer should be contemplated. But the authoritarian visitor insists it be done his or her way.

Where prayer might be an appropriate offering, an enquiry such as "Would you like me to pray with you today or some other time?" is fitting. This saves embarrassment and gives the patient the freedom to say "Some other time."

Even so, the patient may feel guilty in refusing. If this is likely, a further release clause is possible: "Sometimes the last thing we want to do is to pray. God understands when we feel like that. It's okay if you don't desire me to pray."

2. Praying only when asked

This tradition is the easy way to fulfill the responsibility of being tuned in to the patient.

It avoids the awkwardness of not knowing what to pray. You meet a person whose child is in intensive care with severe brain damage. Or maybe a man in his forties with leukemia or HIV/AIDS. What and how do you pray in such circumstances? To be able to pray, or to know if prayer is needed, requires a lot of concentration on what the person is feeling. What if the patient is withdrawn and the relatives are doing the talking?

Do you respond more to the relatives' needs or the patient's desires? If there is no request for prayer, the policy of praying only when asked lets the pastoral visitor off the hook.

There would be many an occasion when the patient and family would welcome the support and comfort that a few well-chosen words of prayer bring.

HIV/AIDS patients, irrespective of the manner in which they contracted the disease, often have an overwhelming sense of ostracism and rejection that is real and hurting. Church folk in particular may be ignorant and judgmental when it comes to the question of HIV/AIDS. For such patients, to be accepted by the pastoral visitor is unbelievably reassuring and spirit-boosting. For some, a prayer to God on their behalf can promote faith in God and the church. It may require a little initiative on the part of the visitor to assess the possible acceptability of prayer and then make an open-ended offer.

It avoids embarrassment. The embarrassment of having an offer of prayer refused extends both to the visitor and the patient. To refuse someone from the church is a courageous thing to do. The possibility of being labeled and branded by the church is likely if the carer reports back to the pastoral care group. Usually the patient knows this. Some patients, of course, do this to test the sincerity of the pastoral visitor. If genuine, the pastoral visitor will come back again and again, quite unperturbed by the refusal.

All the same, pastoral visitors do not expect to be refused. In their own opinion they are making a sacrifice in visiting the hospital and may feel hurt and rejected and look upon the patient as an ingrate. This, of course, does not add to the confidence or the willingness of people to remain in pastoral care ministry.

It avoids dishonesty in praying. Some sections of charismatic and pentecostal movements place a priority of emphasis upon the ministry of healing. A pastoral visitor is expected to pray for healing and a complete cure.

There are also unchurched families. Their language and behavior indicate their irreligious stance. Yet these people, as patients, often welcome the pastoral worker as if they were staunch believers. The pastoral care worker may be faced with the need to minister to them and may be expected by the family to do so, almost as though to provide and ensure a place at the heavenly table.

The need to care for all people with all sorts of expectations is acknowledged, but your ability to fulfill all those expectations is not realistic.

Calls come sometimes in the early hours of the morning to say that a patient has died and the relatives are not coming in but they would like a chaplain or pastoral worker to go and offer a prayer over the body. These requests often have an ulterior motive: They are meant to assuage the relatives' guilt over not coming in themselves.

Integrity and honesty must be maintained. Where prayer has not been requested but it is evident that it is expected, it must be offered sincerely and in faith. Many a time I have been expected to pray for a miracle, which I believed I could not do with a clear conscience. I have also been expected to give a one-way ticket to heaven by prayer! These pathways I have declined, offering prayer for what I could honestly present to God.

Prayers may be said for strength to cope with whatever may happen in the next few days, or that the patient may reach up to God seeking the peace which God alone can give, or that inner healing may be experienced, or that patience may be given to bear the pain or that relief may come from the unbearable.

There are times when I am comfortable in praying for healing. Such prayers are offered when I can pray with integrity. It emphasizes *listening and understanding.*

Listening and understanding may help the patient or relatives to modify some of their attitudes and perceptions, thus easing some of their tensions.

Pastoral care where possible should not stop there, however. Soulen categorically states that prayer is invariably appreciated, but experience compels me to disagree. A more accurate statement would be "prayer is in most cases appreciated." But I do agree with Soulen when he says: *"It [prayer] should arise, whether expressly requested or not, out of the natural development; if it does not, then it should never be forced."* [3]

There are times, as he acknowledges, when prayer is not requested but is the natural progression in the pastoral visit The blanket ban—that unless it is requested there should be no prayer—truncates what might have developed into a fruitful faith ministry in the life of the patient. The patient's expectations may be dashed. Doubts about the visitor's own motivations in hospital visitation may be raised, alongside the question of the visitor's spiritual qualifications.

The visitor needs to feel free and flexible enough to assess what is happening and respond accordingly. The unshackling from the rigid and inflexible enables her or him to adapt to whatever develops.

Soulen's warning should be underscored: prayer should never be forced.

The question for the pastoral carer in a general hospital is, "How do we know when we should pray?" Here are some clues that may indicate the patient's sympathetic attitude to religion and prayer.

INDICATORS FOR PRAYER

Open talk about prayer. The patient actually mentions prayer. It may be only a simple remark like "there are many people praying for me" or "my daughter goes to church and she has her church praying for me" or "I'm not a religious person but I have prayed since I took ill." It is reasonable to assume that such folk will appreciate an offer for prayer. There may be a rebuff occasionally because of their own embarrassment. It may need to be clearly explained that you will do the praying and they will listen.

On many occasions the patient responds by saying, "I don't know how to pray." This is a good opportunity to say that prayer is simply talking to God. When you pray, you tell God what your gut feelings are. After one such explanation the next day a mother said, "I told God how angry I was with him over my baby's condition. It works. I feel so much better now. It seems as if I know God now." Often people are reticent to pray because of anger toward God.

Christian literature at the bedside. A Bible, a daily Bible study program, Christian magazines or other Christian literature on the bedside table indicate a person's active Christian life. Such people seldom refuse the offer of prayer. In fact they often anticipate it.

There are occasions, however, when such literature may lead to a misunderstanding. A religious mother or neighbor, concerned about the patient's spiritual welfare, may have piled up this material, hoping that the loved one might (with time on his or her hands) pick it up, read it and be converted. Such pressure stirs antagonism against religious people so that you may have to work harder to earn the confidence of the patient. Before any consideration of prayer, that literature may become the focal point at some stage of the visit. If there are indications of embarrassment or uneasiness, then drop the subject and avoid the suggestion of prayer until, if ever, the appropriate time arrives.

It is for this reason that I have emphasized *observation* when you first enter the ward. On your next visit you may find that the Christian literature has been put out of sight. This indicates that the shutters are still up for any religious talk or prayer. In such cases it will be your continuing acceptance of the patient as a person and not as a possible church statistic that may prove most fruitful.

Some religious conversation. Irregular or nominal church persons often welcome a visit, if they are not overwhelmed with visitors. Expect the possibility of a range of excuses for not being regular in church attendance. They may declare their faith and even remark that they have said to their spouse they must start going to church again now that the children are older. Such expressions help to relieve their own guilt feelings over their religious inactivity. It is unwise, however, to accept such talk as evidence that prayer is desired.

Hospitalization can provoke sincere consideration of where a person is at spiritually. Initially it may not be overtly expressed. The occasional, if not surreptitious, probing enquiry (sometimes relating to a hypothetical friend) is made. Such probes must be taken seriously and dealt with honestly and meaningfully for the patient. Discernment is required as to the opportune time to offer prayer as it is seldom asked for. The offer made too soon may stifle the search. It is in such circumstances that we must hold our balance.

Religious earnestness must be tempered by patient judgment of the developing dynamics.

Because of the ready conversation of other people on spiritual matters, you automatically know, of course, they would appreciate prayer. In such cases it is expected and desired. But there are those who would prefer someone from their own cultural background or denomination to pray.

With the exceptions noted, patient-initiated, uninhibited religious conversations are generally a good indication of the suitability of offering prayer.

Sharing of an immediate anxiety. Some, whether religious or not, have deep-seated problems or anxieties. Being a person representing the church, you are considered to be trustworthy and able to keep what is said in confidence. Your identification with the church presupposes that you have some access to God. The situation may require more than human solution. When it has been explicitly revealed, an offer of prayer may be accepted or the patient may simply request you to "remember it in your own prayers." The latter response is often from a religiously nonactive person. If such a request has been made, you need to comply because the patient will certainly enquire as to whether you've kept your promise!

Information from family or staff. There are times when the patient is so low or in such deep distress that he or she opens up to the nearest person, such as relatives, nurses, doctors, or other hospital staff. Some of these worries may pertain to spiritual issues. The relatives or staff may express these matters to you, asking if you would be able to take them up or try to have the patient talk about them. When such circumstances arise, always ascertain if the patient's permission was received to relay the matter of the conversation. If such permission was not given, either ask the informant to seek such approval or go to the patient as if nothing has been said, while at the same time trying to provoke discussion in the area of concern.

The information received from the relatives and corroborated by the patient may give sufficient opening for prayer to be offered, even if not requested.

Spiritual intuition. I hesitate to list this indicator. It relies solely on the carer's personal relationship with God. I firmly believe that hospital ministry is one that requires a heavy dependence upon awareness and direction from the Holy Spirit.

Unfortunately, such direction is claimed by many who are more eager to prove their spirituality and right living before others. The Spirit has been held responsible for too many questionable things.

There are times when you become highly sensitive to an inner prompting to introduce the spiritual dimension and prayer to patients. These times I like to call "holy moments." They are not everyday events, although some people would claim such experiences as being common occurrences. Holy moments are reserved for those times when human wisdom is notably unrevealing and when it is difficult to know whether prayer or other spiritual ministration is required. The holy moment of Holy Spirit inspiration is a cherished privilege coming at the exact moment of need.

When one or more of the above indicators are recognized, the question is, "How do I pray?"

HOW TO PRAY

There are several basic rules to be kept in mind. The first and most important one is:

Be brief. Seriously ill patients have a short concentration span. The prayer with such patients should be only thirty seconds to one minute. That allows for no flowery introduction to God. The Lord knows who the patient is and doesn't need to be told at such a time. The petition should be short and direct so that the patient will be able to understand. The prayers for patients not so seriously ill may be longer but kept meaningful and relevant.

A minister's family had been called to his bedside as death was imminent. A senior minister arrived with the family and offered prayer. This good man gave a recital to God of the patient's Christian service and repeatedly thanked God for his life. With eyes closed the senior minister prayed for almost ten minutes, completely unaware of the effect the strain of concentration was having on the patient. The family watched their loved one's weakening, painful struggle. The chaplain and the nursing unit manager behind the glass screen of the nurses' station watched and were about to intervene when the prayer stopped.

The good man died a few minutes later, having undergone stress that he should not have experienced. The senior minister made it obvious that he felt good about having prayed with his colleague just before he died and at having been able to "minister" to the family at such a time.

Pastoral care workers are often oblivious of the added strains and burdens they heap upon a patient, as in this case, because of insensitive and inappropriate behavior.

Mention the patient's name and the names of relevant associates. The patient is often traumatized. The essential concerns are his or her own personal welfare and that of loved ones and close friends. When a person is heavily sedated, often only the names register and nothing else about the prayer. To hear those names means that all are brought under the umbrella of God's care. This is most comforting. Generalizations are irrelevant, meaningless and counterproductive at such times.

Summarize the salient points of the encounter. This should be done without interpreting or running contrary to the feelings of the patient. The prayer at the bedside is incarnational prayer. You are praying the prayer that patients cannot pray for themselves because of their weakened powers of concentration. "Incarnational praying" means that the patient's mind and thoughts are being born in you and presented to God. This highlights the need to listen to the patient and the relatives without a personal commentary on what you think is going on.

Words such as "Lord, you know how (name) feels about what is happening to him or her" or "(name) has expressed the desire to quickly pass into your presence. Hear (name's) cry at this time" or "(name) has been talking about his son (son's name) who seems far from you. (Name) wants him and his wife (wife's name if known) and their children to be under your care" and so on. The emphasis is upon what the patient has expressed in the conversation.

This ability to reflect the patient's mind back to God exactly as expressed proves to the patient that:

- you were listening
- you understood
- you accepted the patient's feelings
- you shared in those feelings
- your concern for the patient is sincere
- you have empathized
- you truly demonstrated pastoral care

Avoid trying to put into the patient's mind anything that is not there. In contrast to the above there are those visitors who do not agree with all the patient's theology and feelings, and they try to use the prayer to put the patient or the relatives straight on a few points. To expect a person to assent to a prayer with which they cannot agree is the easiest way to invite rejection and build tension.

Avoid religious jargon. Bedside praying needs to be simple, in plain understandable language. The religious jargon of previous generations is not understood. The words may carry the meaning of the King James era (A.D.1610) and have different connotations today. It is most probable that any relatives present have not used such words for decades, if ever. Idiomatic language of today conveys the meaning more appropriately, without ambiguity. The use of simple colloquial language equates you with the patient. An air of "down to earth" reality and meaning is engendered by using everyday language.

Bring a sense of God's compassion. What is the purpose of prayer at the bedside? It has many facets. It presents patients' feelings to God so that they have a sense of relief that their feelings have been expressed. But this is insufficient. Patients need to feel that God's concern, love and compassion are available to them.

To know that the future—which is clouded due to a diagnosis, a test, surgery, or a psychiatric drug or radiological treatment—is somehow being watched over by a loving God is one of the greatest comforts and assurances that a patient may receive. That is consolidated when the prayer includes reference to the doctors and staff. Bringing an awareness of the presence of a compassionate God is one of the main purposes of the bedside prayer.

Encourage hope. A person without hope becomes suffocated by a forlorn feeling. His or her condition usually deteriorates very rapidly. The pain and physical distress appear to become more intense. The patient withdraws even further. The pastoral care person seems almost to mock this individual by her or his righteous, healthy presence.

Prayer should encourage hope. Here the prayers must be nothing less than honest, not encouraging false hope. Paul Irion suggests that in cases where a patient has been told that it is a matter of days, hope may be expressed for some good days with pain control, and the support of staff, relatives, friends. He adds that a "deepening faith" is integral to this.[4]

There are times when prayers for physical healing are valid. I have prayed for healing of the body and the Holy Spirit has responded positively. I refer to healings that cannot be classified as psychological. But these occasions are rare. Many petitions for physical healing have not brought the same result. A healing prayer should only be offered when you have a strong inner spiritual conviction that such a prayer must be made.

Dobihal and Stewart see hope as distinct from wishing for better circumstances. Wishing is a passive emotion and not hope. Hope, they say, *"is a goal-directed vision that enables one to live effectively in the present and move trustingly toward future possibilities."*[5] Hope for a physical restoration that has become unrealistic can be turned into expectation of a new and better relationship and experience with God. Prayer, as well as the conversation before (if appropriate), should speak of and include such possibilities. The vision or hope must have some solid grounding in reality. Patients instantly express appreciation for prayers that provide realistic hopes.

Care with words and information. Be careful not to divulge privileged information that staff may have conveyed to you. Care should also be taken not to misread or exaggerate the patient's condition. Depressing wrong impressions may be conveyed by the prayer, including too many words about being "in glory with God." The patient may be denying the seriousness of the condition or there may have been no suggestion and no reason for thinking of death. Under such circumstances to mention eternal peace and glory, or even heaven's anticipation, may give rise to despair, depression and mistrust of relatives and staff because it is assumed that the real condition is being kept from the patient. Patients have lost their will to survive, become a difficult management problem and slowly deteriorated for no medically apparent reason, following a pastoral carer's prayer.

Manipulative prayer is unethical. If the zealousness of some pastoral care workers to see the patient "right with God" before they die becomes the motive for praying, prayer becomes a manipulative tool to obtain their confession and commitment to God. It is blatantly dishonest and unethical. Its effect upon the patient is to increase hostility. For a cardiac patient, in particular, it can raise stress levels and affect blood pressure, predisposing a premature fatal episode. Time that might have been available to the patient to face spiritual issues has been sacrificed because of evangelical enthusiasm.

Breath prayer for the seriously ill. Ron DelBene has produced a helpful series of resource booklets (published by The Upper Room). In these he

introduces "Breath Prayer." His method is to se-
lect a word or phrase expressing need and a fa-
vorite name of God. Those two combined into a
sentence prayer and repeated throughout the day
become a source of great comfort and strength. I
have found this to be of immense value to seriously ill patients whose powers of concentration
are limited. The following are examples of
"Breath Prayers":

- "Dear Savior, ease my pain."
- "Be close to me, loving God."
- "Gentle Jesus, touch my body and spirit."
- "Glorious Father, fill me with peace."

Patients may carry such prayers with them
throughout the day or for several days.

The blessing prayer. In many bedside situations I have no lead as to the patient's religious
affiliations, activities or feelings. No indication of
any kind has been conveyed as to her or his desire for prayer or otherwise.

In such cases I simply use a blessing prayer:
Touching the patient, on the hand or arm for example, I depart with the simple words, "God be
with you" or "May God bless you." On numer-
ous occasions the next visit has elicited words

like "You don't know how much your touch and blessing meant to me when you left." One patient claimed being healed through it. Scans later that day showed no signs of the suspected diagnosis. Pain and the other symptoms did not recur from the moment of that spoken blessing.

The short four-word blessing may be the most effective prayer you can offer. It is also not intrusive upon the privacy or the stance of the patient. It can be accepted or ignored without adverse reaction toward the pastoral visitor. The patient can be comfortable with it in front of nonreligious visitors. This blessing prayer I invoke on almost every patient I visit. It needs to be offered sincerely and not simply as a farewell line.

Prayer is an important aspect of ministry at the bedside. On many occasions when I have prayed, trying to give the patient permission to let go and be free to die, the patient has actually died during the prayer with my hand on the forehead or other appropriate part of the body—all in about a minute. On the other hand, prayers of hope have lifted patients to fight for life. Prayer is one of the most important communication networks available to us all and must be used lovingly and correctly.

Kubler-Ross wrote:

What amazed me was the number of clergy who felt quite comfortable using a prayer book or chapter from the Bible as the sole communication between them and the patients, thus avoiding listening to their needs and being exposed to questions they might be unable or unwilling to answer.[6]

Sometimes it would be wiser to leave your prayer book at home. It often makes the prayer irrelevant and impersonal. It is highly unlikely that the prayer read will equate with the needs of any particular patient. Unless the prayer is centered upon the patient and his or her needs, emotions and hopes, it is of little consequence. The prayer must also affirm God's caring love, concern, and vital interest in the patient.

To balance the above there are some folk who are more comfortable with the old, tried and familiar liturgies. They would be lost without them. Often they are able to recite them with the priest. That ability to do so brings immeasurable comfort. They feel the church of history is with them and functioning for them in their need. For them the prayer liturgies are immensely valuable and we should not deny them. Of course, with the diminishing percentage of active churchgoers the number of patients familiar with such liturgy is also decreasing. Therefore, it is essential again to become aware of the patient's needs concerning prayer. Prayer always must be for patients in a form that is not only acceptable to them, but in which they can participate and respond.

Bedside prayer ministry requires a developing sensitivity to where a patient is, a deepening intimacy between you and your God and a growing ability to utilize these in tandem.

NOTES

1. Kent D. Richmond, *Preaching to Sufferers: God and the Problem of Pain*, 91–96.

2. Lloyd M. Perry and Charles M. Sell, *Speaking to Life's Problems*, 111.

3. Richard N. Soulen et al., *Care for the Dying*, 55.

4. Paul E. Irion, *Hospice and Ministry*, 102.

5. Edward F. Dobihal, Jr., and Charles William Stewart, *When a Friend Is Dying: A Guide to Caring for the Terminally Ill and Bereaved*, 84.

6. Elisabeth Kubler-Ross, *On Death and Dying: What the Dying Have to Teach Doctors, Nurses, Clergy, and Their Own Families*, 118.

⇥ CHAPTER 5 ⇤

Jesus—A Theological Model

Pastoral care in the hospital is not a ministry for the person who is looking for something to do, who wants to just feel accepted within the church, who sees it as a means of fulfilling personal needs, who uses it as an escape from unresolved personal problems, or who is merely eager to please God. Hospital ministry is as much a call of God to a specific area of Christian service as is a call into the ordained ministry, a religious order or a missionary challenge. A person so called must clearly possess a theology of hospital visitation.

Any call into Christian service, either clerical or lay, requires a theological perception and motivation. This provides the foundation and stability that helps to shape the character, the approach and the dedication to the task. When a person receives a phone call from a friend to come for a visit, that person's busy routine is not dropped unless there is some definite sense of urgency that demands an altered schedule. Theology provides the criteria whereby each situation is assessed and action taken. It determines the attitude the carer should have toward the patient and the situation of the patient.

If a theology of Christian pastoral care is to have any real validity, it must find its roots in the person and work of Jesus Christ. Peter (1 Peter 3:12–19) tells us that Jesus, by his own suffering, set the example as to how to cope with the suffering of persecution. Paul and the writer to the Hebrews, along with others, develop theology that set us the pattern for service. In this chapter we will look in more detail at the example Jesus set. This is meant to be the launching pad for pastoral care theology.

There are so many outstanding features of Jesus' life that it would be improper to consider any theological development prioritized according to the place of its appearance in this chapter. Jesus keeps all things in fine balance. His theological perspectives are so interwoven that they form a whole, each in its place, requiring its own due consideration and practice.

Here we shall pursue eleven facets of Jesus' theology of pastoral care as taught and demonstrated by him. We could turn to other Scriptures and see further aspects. The treatment of these dimensions of Jesus' theology is intended to be a springboard to stimulate your own thinking. These aspects could also be termed catalysts that will be a means of developing and enriching your understanding of God and his expectations of us as people involved in pastoral care.

Theology is never static. Our every new experience of life, we should reflect upon and learn from. If a person's theological perceptions are not developing, it is likely that he or she will not be suitable as a pastoral visitor to hospitals. His or her God is likely to be too small to cope with the number and type of situations the visitor will encounter. An expanding theology reveals a bigger, more wonderful God than was experienced before.

New discoveries about God provide the confidence, excitement and resources to be wise, caring, firm and yet gentle, as Christ was, in dealing with patients.

A THEOLOGY
OF ACCEPTANCE

Any cursory reading of the gospels will bring astonishment at the types of people Jesus associated with. This factor was one of the great weapons his enemies wielded against Jesus. He came basically for the needy, and in particular those who were lost and helpless in their own quagmires. Jesus himself said that he came to heal the sick and not the well. He had come not to call respectable people but outcasts (Matthew 9:12–13). This was the response to the Pharisees' questioning of his eating with Matthew and the tax collectors. The Samaritan woman (John 4) was not only a Samaritan but also a woman and a harlot. His society dictated that he should not speak to her; but in full acceptance of her as a needy person, he spoke directly to her about the troublesome areas of her life.

Zaccheus was a person hated by society and distrusted because of his cheating and fraudulent extraction of tax from people. It was not only because of his smallness of stature that he climbed the tree. He wanted to see Jesus and knew he wouldn't be allowed to mingle in peace on the street with the other villagers. A tree provided

cover for him to fulfill his desire. Jesus not only
accepted Zaccheus in front of the crowd, he identified himself with him by eating in his house
(Luke 19:1–10).

In those times, an adulteress was automatically stoned to death upon exposure. Jesus, in a re-
markable fashion, not only received such a
woman, but sent her away forgiven (John 8:11).
He highlighted the unacceptability of Gentiles to
the Jews when the Syrian woman from Phoeni-
cia approached him for the healing of her daughter from demon possession, but after witnessing
her determined faith in him, he accepted her and
her prayer was fulfilled (Mark 7:25–31).

For another example, we could turn to the
man of Gadara who was banished to the cemetery because of his hideous, uncontrollable
manic behavior. He was healed by Jesus. Again,
although lepers were the untouchables of his day,
Jesus not only cured them, he touched them,
breaking the law and convention in doing so.
The touching (above all the other things he did)
reinforced the fact of his acceptance of them as
they were. (See Leviticus 13, 14, Matthew 8:1–4.)

None were more despised by the Jews than
the Roman soldiers, yet Jesus had no hesitation
in listening to the plea from the Roman centuri-

on to heal his servant. He graciously accepted him and acceded to his prayer (Matthew 8:5–13).

Jesus was unrestricted and unrestrained in his reaching out to needy people, relieving them of their burdens. He did not consider breeding, background or social status. Whoever they were and of whatever faith, Jesus accepted them. The ministry of a pastoral care person means moving out to accept the patient, resident, family or staff—whoever they are and whatever their ethnic background, religion and state of need.

A THEOLOGY OF AVAILABILITY

Matthew tells us that Jesus, when told of the death of his cousin, John the Baptist, went by boat to the other side of the lake. This presumably was to escape the crowds, to be alone to grieve and no doubt to consider the implications of John's death for his own ministry. The crowds followed him around the lake, so he was forced to teach and heal the whole day. At the end of an exhausting day the people were tired, hungry and had a long trek back home. It would have been easy for Jesus to have dismissed them and pursued the privacy he desired. Instead he fed that great crowd with the five loaves and two fish. Jesus, in spite of the circumstances, made himself available to the people, who had physical, medical and spiritual needs (Matthew 14:1–21).

That availability is seen when he was moving along with a great crowd of people, healing and teaching. Jairus, the ruler of the synagogue, sought Jesus' assistance to heal his ailing daughter. Jesus could have easily said that he was too busy healing scores of people, and what priority did a twelve-year-old girl have over these others? Yet he deliberately made himself available. His reach extended out to even the insignificant members of society (Mark 5:22–43). This is again exemplified when the disciples tried to prevent mothers bringing their children for Jesus to bless. He stopped his teaching, took these children in his arms and blessed them (Mark 10:13–16). The message of Jesus' life and ministry is a call for his disciples of all ages to be ready and available to all people.

A THEOLOGY OF ACCOUNTABILITY

Matthew, Mark and Luke each record Jesus' startlingly dramatic words, spoken after Peter's wa-

tershed confession of him as the Messiah. Those
words, which he reiterated several times later,
showed plainly how he must suffer, die and rise
again (Matthew 16:21–23; Mark 8:31–33; Luke
9:22). On each occasion, an imperative is used:
"Jesus must. . . ." The disciples tried to dissuade
him (Matthew 16:22), but the determination was
there. That determination may be gauged by the
sense of accountability and responsibility expressed by Jesus himself in his reflection on the
Good Shepherd. This is teaching which he applied to himself (John 10). The Good Shepherd is
responsible for the safety of the sheep and is accountable to the owner of the sheep for their se-
curity. The Good Shepherd's accountability reaches as far as the sacrifice of his own life.

This Jesus, who must have known the extent
of the suffering to be endured on Calvary, shrank
from the reality of the physical and spiritual trau-
ma to be borne. Gethsemane reveals the intensi-
ty of this struggle of Jesus (Matthew 26:36–46).

People called into hospital visitation accept a
sense of accountability to God for those entrust-
ed to them in this ministry. A half-hearted or in-
different commitment to this form of pastoral
care indicates a failure to fully accept responsibility for the patients, relatives or staff. The main-

tenance of an accountability framework rescues the carer from self-pity and self-pampering. The spirit of responsibility is evident in the boy Jesus' reply to his parents in the temple: "Didn't you know that I had to be in my Father's house?"

A THEOLOGY OF CARE

The one defining characteristic of Jesus' life is that of care. He showed compassion, concern and empathy in all his dealings with everyone. The implication and scope of this for chaplains is in his famous "judgment scene" (Matthew 25:31–46), which so clearly and specifically declares that unless we have shown true care of the remotest needy person in our society then we are not fit for God's kingdom. The parables of the lost sheep and the lost coin (Luke 15) indicate a certain persistence in the caring until the final discovery is made or the task completed. In other words, Jesus considered the thoroughness of the care to be crucial.

Jesus was continually moved to compassion. "As he saw the crowds, he was filled with pity for them because they were worried and helpless, like sheep without a shepherd" (Matthew 9:36). The same caring concern resulted in his feeding of the four thousand. He saw that having been without food for three days they might feel faint on the way home (Matthew 15:32).

The principal characteristic of Jesus' caring ministry was this persistence in completing the task of caring. The demonic man in the cemetery at Gadara, an uncontrollable maniac, abandoned by society, found deliverance because Jesus was not repelled by his appalling state (Mark 5:1–13).

Turning again to the woman at the well, we find that she initially questioned Jesus' right to talk with her and rebuffed him. He saw her need. He broke cultural mores to meet her on her own ground. When she changed the subject, making it a religious issue, to take the spotlight off her own sorry plight, he persisted until she embraced the truth about herself and about him (John 4:1–26).

In both these cases, Jesus saw through to completion the task of caring. The swine careering into the sea to drown provided evidence for the maniacally possessed demonic that he might have the confidence of a new freedom from the fear of demons. The satisfaction of seeing a social outcast come to a belief in him as the Messiah took precedence over Jesus' need to eat (John 4:31–34).

The provision of care for isolated, suffering, emotionally hurting or otherwise disturbed people was the sincere motivation Jesus evidenced throughout the whole of his earthly ministry. The first temptation after his baptism, and his repeated command to beneficiaries to tell no one who had performed the miracle on them, is sufficient indication that Jesus was not using his caring acts to manipulate people into the kingdom. In many cases those acts bore fruit of eternal and spiritual significance, but it appears that the majority of those blessed by Jesus' caring did not pursue a deeper spiritual involvement. Jesus, out of his caring compassion, responded naturally without imposing any conditions.

That same concern, which results in action to alleviate the need, should be the characteristic of the pastoral person and the visitor. Other motives, evangelical or denominational priorities, kill the true spirit of caring. The hidden agenda becomes patently obvious to the one offered the assistance. The care of Jesus was offered out of his own reaction to the less-than-whole life experienced by others. He ministered without preconditions or strings attached. His caring action bore its own fruit.

A THEOLOGY OF
SENSITIVITY

It is easy to recognize some needs. It is a different proposition to be sensitive to the other peculiar, and seemingly insignificant, needs that ultimately may be most important to the person. This singularly important gift of sensitivity is evident when Jesus restored life to Jairus's daughter. The excitement and joy of an unbelievable miracle overshadowed all sensitivity to the girl's real need. She had been starved for several days because of her condition. She was weak. It took Jesus to tell them that she needed some bodily nourishment. "Give her something to eat" (Mark 5:43).

Mary the sister of Lazarus, who may have been Mary Magdalene (Mary of Bethany and Mary of Magdala never appear together in any of the gospel events), gave a spectacular and extravagant display of adoration at a dinner in the home of Lazarus. She massaged expensive ointment worth several years' wages for an average person into the feet of Jesus. Judas's strong criticism of him for permitting that seeming waste was rebuffed by Jesus. Jesus sensitively looked deep into the heart of Mary, perceiving the force behind such a display of devotion. He saw that any rejection of that act would have left lasting hurt. Her purity of motive was sensitively applauded rather than squashed by Jesus (John 12:7).

To cite another example: One can only remotely imagine the shame, remorse and disgust of Peter when he heard the cock crow after he had denied his Master. The sensitive Jesus recognized the need to forgive and heal the tortured Peter. A patronizing response of forgiveness would have left Peter squirming more. Jesus, by his threefold demand of affirmation of love, made it difficult for Peter not to be reminded of his three denials (John 21:15–19). Without that replay of his darkest hour and without the threefold affirmation of love, forgiveness and commission to feed the lambs and sheep, Peter would have probably remained a maimed, guilt-ridden disciple rather than becoming the fierce apostle.

Jesus always delved below the surface to understand innermost feelings and observe the slightest trace of camouflaged need. Pastoral carers must ceaselessly be alert to such need, sharpening their skills of sensitivity until the other person becomes aware of Christlike perceptiveness. Verbal and nonverbal communication, with their various subtleties, must be constantly interpreted with precision, after the pattern of Jesus.

A THEOLOGY OF OBEDIENCE

From Isaiah on through the whole New Testament, we read of the Messiah being sent by God to heal and to save (Isaiah 61:1, John 3:16, Galatians 4:4, 1 John 4:9). Jesus' incarnation was for the sole purpose of human salvation. His life and ministry were consistent with full obedience to that commission. He did not shrink from it. He held himself accountable to God and this accountability was fulfilled through his complete obedience.

As a twelve-year-old in the temple, he showed awareness of his mission (Luke 2:41–50) and sought knowledge to equip himself to obediently fulfill it. In his adult life, his disciples persistently tried to squash his talk of going to Jerusalem to die. When Peter objected at Caesarea Philippi, Jesus accused him of being Satan's instrument of temptation to divert him from the path of obedience.

There were so many things Jesus could have done to avert the crucifixion. He need not have gone to Jerusalem for the Passover. He could have called down twelve legions of angels (Matthew 26:52–54). It would have been easy to slip into the darkness of Olivet when he saw the crowd coming out of the city gate to arrest him. He could have compelled Judas to stay in the upper room and not report to the Sanhedrin. Clearly, Jesus had every opportunity to avoid Calvary. His commitment to his divine commission took precedence over the fear of what he knew he had to endure.

It is with the same sense of commitment that we should fill the commission that Christ has given to us to minister to those ill in bed. Paul (Ephesians 4:9–16) tells of Jesus giving to each of us separate gifts for ministry and for the smooth functioning of the body of Christ, the church. Those gifts are given in order that the ministry that the Lord has assigned to each individual Christian may be obediently fulfilled.

Without a call to a hospital ministry, the necessary gifts for such ministry may be absent. Without such a call, there can be no obedience in such service. It becomes a need fulfillment or an activity adopted merely through a sense of duty. Obedience can only follow a commissioning such as Christ received from the Father (John 3:16). Examine the extent of the divine initiative behind your involvement in hospital ministry. Whether clergy or lay, we need to be assured that we are endeavoring to minister in God's place, in his time, and in his way, so that our ministry may be truly a ministry obedient to the divine command.

A hospital visitor is one who is called by God to enter a situation where there are numbers of hurting humanity. We are to approach them with the sense of urgency and compassion that Jesus' example, in sincere obedience to the divine command, set before us.

A THEOLOGY OF WITNESS

It is true that the great commission of Jesus to his church was to preach, teach and baptize all nations (Matthew 28:19-20). It is also true that he said on his ascension day that his followers were to be witnesses. Witnessing may take many forms. It may be through the spoken word. Often preaching is most effective, as we see in the way the masses clung to the teaching of Jesus. Yet it has been true over the centuries that many have been won over to Christ through merely observing the life pattern of a Christian. The thief on the cross found salvation, not through Jesus' preaching, but by observing him dying and observing his love and compassion even in death—"Father, forgive them"—"Mother, behold your Son" (Luke 23, John 19). The Roman centurion at the cross was able to say, "Truly this man was a righteous man" (Luke 23:47–48).

Jesus made clear the meaning of witness when he spoke of it being as "light" or "salt" (Matthew 5:13–16). A hospital visitor who walks the corridors of the institution must be seen as a light that enlightens all patients, residents, relatives and staff. The aura is one that attracts, not to the carer as a person, but to the Christ whom he or she represents. The Master's touch is spread by pastoral visitors to those who cross their path. This is effective witness that builds the eternal kingdom.

A THEOLOGY OF SERVANTHOOD

One of the major reasons for the nonrecognition of Jesus as the Christ by the Jews was their failure to identify Isaiah's servant passages in messianic context. Jesus in all respects fulfilled the servant role of that prophet. When Zebedee's wife claimed for her sons positions of preeminence in Christ's kingdom, he replied by stressing the role of servanthood. He said of himself that he had not come to be waited upon but to serve and to give his life for others (Matthew

20:28). The concept of servanthood in action is never more clearly seen than in the upper room where he washed his disciples' feet (John 13: 1-17). Jesus proclaimed his act as an example that they must put into practice. No messenger is greater than the master.

Jesus by reason of his divine nature, had the right to live in opulence and grandeur, with a retinue to serve him. Yet his lifestyle was the opposite of this expectation. No fixed abode—today he would have been declared a vagrant. Being at the beck and call of the influential and the poor, he served them by offering them a service that no one else could provide. The lepers, synagogue rulers, army captains, fishermen, the wealthy (for example, Nicodemus and Joseph of Arimathaea), tax gatherers, and housewives all accepted his services without any obligation.

His servanthood was offered to all without fear or prejudice, without conditions and without fanfare. The service he offered was given to the grateful leper and the nine ungrateful lepers (Luke 17:11-19). The Pharisees and the prostitutes met him on common ground (Luke 7:36-50). Whether it was spiritual (John 3:1-21) or a desperate physical disability (John 5:1-9), Jesus offered the needed service. As the teacher supreme (Matthew 5–7; and John 13–17) or as the blesser of babies (Matthew 19:13–15), Jesus observed no age preferences. His servanthood was unrestricted—to believer and non-Jew alike. It showed no bias. It was servanthood at its most menial yet noblest. It was versatile enough to meet the smallest and the most traumatic crises of life.

It is therefore incumbent upon us to emulate this servant role. Regretfully, we can be selective in our hospital ministry; there are few of us who can claim to have never been discriminating in our servanthood. It is easier to minister to someone with whom we have a natural rapport. Yet the others with less appealing personalities or backgrounds most probably are in more need of our services than those who are well supported and popular.

Jesus set the example so that we should follow in his footsteps and be a servant of all.

A THEOLOGY OF LOVE

No look at Jesus should omit the patently obvious key to his whole life and teaching—the theology of love. "For God so loved the world that he gave . . ." (John 3:16), for the casual Scripture reader, seems to say that it was all the Father's love, that Jesus just meekly acquiesced. But it took Jesus' love to see its fulfillment. If we consider the coequality and unity of the Godhead, then love also is equally determined. Without Jesus' full commitment to love there would have been no atonement. The whole of Jesus' ministry was a continuous kaleidoscope of love and compassion. The healings, the teachings, the acceptance of gross injustice and humiliation, and the infinite patience are all demonstrations of his great love.

The message of the Good Samaritan (Luke 10:30–37) urges us to love our neighbor as ourselves. The Good Shepherd suggests a love that leads to the supreme sacrifice (John 10:11). Jesus reduced the divine commands to two from which all right living surges forth—Love God and love your neighbor (Luke 10:27). John's Gospel and John's letters immortalize the love aspect of Jesus and the expectation that his followers will be identified through love. Love is the base and foundation of all true Christian ministry and service. Paul outlined the quality of this love to be seen in the church (1 Corinthians 13).

Love and empathy should characterize this ministry of the carer. Doing it merely out of duty removes the warmth, spontaneity and integrity from such ministry. Love provides the base on which to build.

A THEOLOGY OF CONFRONTATION

In a rather strange contrast to a theology of sensitivity, acceptance, love and care, when the circumstance required it, Jesus confronted people. Often in the life of the local church or denomination, problems, difficulties, and even schisms occur because in the early days of the dispute, appropriate confrontation does not take place. The matter is allowed to fester until a massive abscess grows and bursts, with disastrous affects on the life and witness of the church. Paul (1 Corinthians 5:1–5) challenged the Corinthian church to deal with a church member involved in an incestuous relationship. The church's lack of courage to confront several issues caused Paul to write letters using strong language.

Jesus, called the "meek and mild," certainly did not behave like a kindly but ineffective individual when he saw wrongdoing and inconsistencies in the lives of people. His sensitiveness to what was going on deep down caused him to speak out strongly against certain individuals and groups.

The Pharisees and scribes were a particularly powerful lobby that he took to task over their false and legalistic teaching (Matthew 23:13–16). We are told of an upright, honest and likable young man, a leader of his people (Luke 18:18–25). Jesus could have extolled his uprightness. His honest seeking after eternal life was sincere when he approached Jesus. Yet Jesus pointed out to him his area of weakness—his love of his estate. He went away sad because he knew Jesus had put his finger on his weak spot. Jesus could confront people when it was necessary.

There were times in Jesus' life when we might feel he should have been firmer. The woman taken in adultery (John 8:1–11) is a case in point. But Jesus felt no need to press the sense of guilt and shame further. To rub more salt into a raw and open heart may be counter-effective. The confrontation came in the words, "Go, sin no more."

Lucy's condition was terminal. One of her daughters had been rebellious in younger years and had broken away from the family. Lucy did not want to see this daughter, Joan. In talking with the family, Joan said she was heartbroken over her mother's stubbornness. She felt she couldn't face the future if her mother died without a reconciliation. Obstinate Lucy, cherishing her Christian code of morality, felt Joan had disgraced God and the family.

Because of her physical distress it was not easy for me to point out to Lucy that Jesus still loved Joan even if her mother didn't. But it had to be done. I assured her that Jesus was prepared to forgive Joan. Why couldn't *she* forgive?

The reunion between those two was a very tearful one. Lucy regained a lost peace and a lost daughter. Joan was rewarded with a mother's love and a mother's forgiveness. Without the confrontation with Lucy, the sadness and heartache would not have been healed.

It is sometimes difficult for patients to face the reality of their condition. Where the attitude is out of the normal character of the person, it may be necessary to bring to bear a little gentle confrontation to restore more sanity to the relationship between the patient and other family members.

There are times when the need for confrontation on spiritual issues arises in the hospital, but visitors who feel it is necessary on every visit to bring a spiritual challenge are ignoring many other factors, such as the patient's physical condition, powers of concentration and the real need for such confrontation. Jesus did not confront on every occasion. Confrontation is a ministry that should be the result of the pastoral visitor's own relationship with God through the Spirit, who directs such a move. This will minimize the risk of rejection and maximize the possibility of fruitfulness, because the timing will be right.

As Jesus discerned when to confront, so must we seek to develop a similar gift of discernment. Notice how at times Jesus sternly, even angrily confronted, as when he overturned the tables of the money changers. On the other hand, he confronted Peter with gentle tenderness at the lakeside breakfast after the resurrection, and opened his hands to Thomas in the upper room to show the nail prints. The method of confrontation must be appropriate to the situation.

Jesus' confrontation with Peter, "Get behind me, Satan," contrasts with his action of breaking bread in the home of the two Emmaus disciples (Luke 24:13–35). This latter action was his way of confronting those two with the facts of his resurrection. There could have been no more effective method of confrontation in the circumstances.

Confrontation is not always a head-on clash. The hospital visitor confronts according to the persons involved, the nature of the circumstances and the possibility of irrevocable, destructive hurt. In the upper room (John 13:21–30) in light of the horrendous act of betrayal, Jesus confronted Judas with the most appealing warning. Again, Jesus becomes our model for confrontation.

A THEOLOGY OF RENEWAL

Jesus spent himself in a caring ministry. Since he was God in human form, it is easy for us to assume that he was able to take the ministry of pastoral care in his stride, with the minimum of physical, emotional or spiritual stress.

As we study the life of Jesus, however, we see that that was not the case. Every miracle drew power from him, as he exclaimed when the woman touched the hem of his garment (Luke 8:46). Mark indicates that following the murder of John the Baptist, Jesus moved the disciples to a place where they could be alone to "rest a while" (Mark 6:31). Jesus recognized the emotional drain that they all had experienced and the need to marshal their forces physically, emotionally and spiritually.

They did not find the opportunity for the planned recuperation and retreat. The crowds followed, and then came the miracle of the feeding of the five thousand. This was another day of teaching and healing and equally draining ministry, so Jesus retired to the mountain to be alone with God (Mark 6:45–47). Six to nine hours later he joined the disciples by walking on the water (Matthew 14:22–25).

Jesus spent many hours of the early morning in prayer with God, renewing himself for the preaching, teaching and healing ministry in Galilee: (Mark 1:35–38). When in Jerusalem it was his habit to retire to the Mount of Olives each night to pray (Luke 22:39).

Genuine pastoral care saps and erodes the physical, emotional and spiritual reserves of carers, who, like Jesus, need to be restored. Without renewal, caring becomes stressful and burdensome. This can lead to burnout and can dramatically reduce the effectiveness of the caring. Efficiency and perceptiveness become lost in the panic to cope with the number of patients, their problems and personal needs.

Burnout does not come with overwork; it is the result of trying to function on drained resources. It is produced when the work is approached in anxiety and stress instead of in the renewed strength gained through recreational, spiritual "time off."

Matthew describes graphically Jesus' encounter with God prior to the arrest and Calvary (Matthew 26:36–46). He made an open honest declaration of his feelings. He shrank from Calvary, he let God know what he thought of it. The communication was frank, open, intimate and spiritually acute. Jesus knew, Jesus accepted, Jesus went forth renewed and strengthened for the battle. The ministry of care continued in spite of his personal distress and anguish as he forgave his tormentors, as he blessed the dying thief and as he provided for his mother. Only a man being constantly renewed by the times spent meeting with God could have continued to persevere in pastoral care under such circumstances (John 19:25–27; Luke 23:39–43).

As pastoral workers, we need to study and follow closely Jesus' lead in this matter, treating as high priority times set aside for renewal.

There are many methods. God can speak through the Scriptures as we reflect upon them. God can reveal himself and his ways as we sit and meditate. God can open spiritual eyes as we move into his natural world and sift the insights that come to us.

Some people find the writing of a daily or weekly journal a way of keeping in healthy perspective the events in which they participate.

Personally, I find that when the stress is heavy, I have to take myself aside and face the confronting issue. As I review it, I set it down on paper in a prayer-poem form. By the time the writing is finished, my whole attitude to the situation is changed. The anxiety has been diffused and I continue the ministry with peace of mind and spirit.

Each week I make time (usually on a Sunday morning) for a reflective, meditative period with God. This fills me with the awareness of our Lord's presence. Invariably it becomes the time of renewal and reequipment for a ministry that will further draw from my spirit and strength until another meeting with him replenishes me.

Pastoral care workers in hospital work need to ensure that periods of renewal are built into their week—not just times of Bible reading and the saying of prayers. There must be an occasion when God in Christ is met and deep communication is experienced. With the intimacy of such renewal encounters as a basis, ministry to people in need becomes an occasion when such people are able to feel that Jesus is coming near to them also.

This theology provides a positive approach to pastoral care. It enables the pastoral visitor to have confidence in:

A *Relevant God,* who is flexible in responding to the needs of his people;

A *Compassionate God,* who cares for the whole person—body, mind and spirit;

A *Compelling God,* to whom the pastoral visitor and his people may turn with confidence, for guidance, wisdom and strength;

A *Suffering God,* who shares humanity's sufferings;

A *Patient God,* who bears with our imperfections and stumblings as we try to serve him;

An *Encouraging God,* who picks us up, comforts us and sends us back into the fray with greater enthusiasm.

In supplement 4 an effort is made to bring this theology into practical perspective because the pure application of a theology may always be distorted or exploited as a manipulative tool, both by the carer and the one to whom care is offered. In hospital ministry this is a real possibility. Work through the issues raised, making relevant applications to your own situation.

Theological Meditations

Living Water

The best laid plans
Are often upturned.
Crises arise, turmoil besets,
The program is abandoned.
A detour, another direction,
A wearisome unwanted journey
Through parts inhospitable.
At least the disciples and Jesus
Knew that they were in alien territory.
Even hallowed Jacob's well
Was not a Jewish sanctuary.

What could have been more deterring?
A Samaritan woman coming
After women's hours to draw water.

She telegraphed by the hour of the day
That she was socially unacceptable.
But Jesus didn't say,
Ho! Hum! Boring,
What a pest,
"She'll disturb the peacefulness."
He looked at this woman.
He loved her in a nonsexual way.
How could he do so?
Knowing her unsavory moral history,
He engaged her in conversation.
How could he do it?
Because he understood.
He was not judgmental.
This Jesus was the God
By whom all things were made.
He was the God of Compassion.
He possessed a love for that woman
That transcended human love.
A love that reaches down
To elevate the jaundiced eye
Off the humiliation and suffering
Imposed upon her
By selfish exploitive men.
A love that sees the inward mind.
That perceives circumstances,

That hears those cries,
"The things my heart would not do, I do."
The things I do, my true spirit would not.
My human actions, I am helpless to control
    myself.

Jesus' gift of love offers a great boon,
A gift that none other can give.
A promise of living water
That will remove the guilt,
Take away the stigma of shame,
Dispatch the fear of more failures,
Give confidence of victory,
Elevate the fallen self esteem,
Heal the woundedness of spirit,
Restore the peace of a righteous heart.
This love is the love
The woman at the well
Accepted as living water.
She drank deeply,
She discovered forgiveness.
She rejoiced in her new blessedness.
She reveled in her newly experienced peace.
Jesus still is sitting at the well.
He knows even me,
Still he stretches out the cup to me.

God's Provision

A Sunday Morning Meditation

Unaware of human eyes they searchingly tread
The verge beneath the gums and casuarinas.
There are grass seeds, perhaps a worm or two.
That seemingly is not their intent.
These two Indian Mynas are selective.
Their yellow ringed eyes and yellow beaks
    coordinate.
Bypassed are leaves and twigs.
A feather or two are picked from the grass.
They pass from quill to tip and then are
    discarded.

Dropped, threadlike, lean and thin,
A casuarina leaf is similarly processed.
Pliable and soft it passes the test.
Together they soar into a tree,
It is springtime; the nest has to be made.
Are the distant sparrows doing the same?
Remember, Lord, when you told us to look
At the birds of the air and the lilies of the field.
You said you would provide for us as you did
    them.
I see it now, Lord! The mynas have all the
    materials provided.

They will never have a nest or a family
Unless they search, examine and test
    expertly.
Then they must weave it into the nest,
To suit the needs of their eggs and offspring.

We must seek and utilize your gifts.
Your provision for mankind is unlimited.
We take it for granted and yet expect more.
The lesson of the mynas is clear.
If I am to experience the optimum
In material and spiritual blessings;
Cooperation with you, perceptive foraging,
Diligent determination and persistent
    endeavor are your ways.

Excite me Lord, to see the possibilities,
In all that you have provided around me.
Let me search, examine, test and weave,
With your provided expertise and wisdom.
May my patients share these gifts
That their lives may be touched and
    strengthened.
Let them see you as the great provider.
To see me is unimportant,
To see you is pacifying and healing.

The joy of sharing

It's late at night,
I've just been around to Accident and
   Emergency.
It was sad to see this thirty-year-old.
She overdosed on drugs prescribed for her
   today.
Then there was the invalid pensioner who
   was finding life hard.
I was able to quieten her a little.

Next I experienced the joy of sharing.
A full-time member of staff has a school age
   family.
She's been feeling the tension between work
   and home.
The financial strain that forced her to work
   no longer bares its teeth.
A part-time job would be ideal,
Particularly one involving the midnight shift.
You've been listening to her, Lord.
She is faithful in her prayer and communion
   with you.
She acknowledges your provision of her
   present job.

This week it was suggested that she apply
    for a new vacancy.
It was for the one job she saw as suitable.
More than for anyone it was tailored for her
    present needs.
In her act of sharing in Christ, she asked,
"I want you to pray for me and this job.
I've got confidence that God is working this
    out."
Her eyes appeared watery as she spoke.
Springs of joy in God were bringing tears of
    gratitude.
It was infectious. You WERE with us.
My eyes filled like hers.

When our hearts are full of God's nearness,
When his assurance floods our lives,
When we share with others our blessings,
Our spirit of joy fills their lives.
Their lives, too, become a hymn of rejoicing.

I suspect, Lord, I'm guilty of denying others.
I do not share as much as I should
My thanksgiving, praise and gratitude to
    you.
It can open the gates of blessing and
    fellowship.

The joy of sharing is unbelievably rewarding
To the person sharing and to the one
    receiving.
Help me to be more unashamedly open in
    my sharing,
To use that sharing for the spiritual advance
    of others.

Examples of Patients' Prayers

The first night in hospital

Tonight, Lord, I feel I am a different person. I can't do as I please. A lot of my independence and freedom have gone. It seems as if I'm a child again. That's not a bad thought to end the day on, a child dependent upon a father. You are my Heavenly Father. That is how you would like it. In sincerity that's how I would like it. Let me sleep tonight comforted in this relationship.

Before an operation

Lord, in a little while I'll be operated on. I have moments when I feel a bit scared. I know I have a good surgeon. I need a peace and assurance that is beyond me. Please be with me so your peace and assurance may be mine.

An exhausting day

It's been a grueling day today, Lord. I feel dopey and exhausted. I'm lost for words. You understand how it is and I love you for it. Just stick close by until I can talk more with you. It gives me strength and encouragement to know you care for me even throughout the night. Thanks for seeing me through today.

Receiving a bad report

What a blow I've been dealt today, Lord. I feel devastated and shattered. I'm lost. I don't know what to say or even think. My plans, my family, my friends, myself—well, just everything is all part of this turmoil. I want to cry. I am angry at the unfairness. Yet I want to tell my family I love them and need them. Deep inside I am so horribly alone, empty and helpless. Lord, look upon me. Lord, come to me as I cry to you. Fill me, Lord, with your understanding. Grip me in your love that I may come to grips with what is happening.

After an operation

Father, I still feel groggy and sore. Yesterday was a big ordeal although I didn't know much about it. Today I feel relief, it's over now. I have a deep sense of gratitude for your loving care and concern shown through all that the doctors and nurses have done. Help me to show my appreciation by my sharing of your Spirit with them.

Irritable

Dear Father, I've felt a bit irritable today. Maybe it's my condition or the treatment or all the tests I'm having. It's not making it easy for the staff or the other patients.

Forgive me, Lord, and just give me that patience and tolerance I need at this time. Help me to be more understanding tomorrow. A good night's rest will be helpful for this. Better still, a consciousness that you are with me all day tomorrow. May it be so, dear Savior.

Encouraged

Oh, my great God, it feels good to be walking around again. I still get tired. It's hard to concentrate for long. These moments when I can think about you and talk with you make things seem so much brighter. In normal life I say I'm too busy to speak with you. May your Spirit together with mine allow me to make the most of this time. Just the thought of your forgiveness, your love, your companionship gives me new purpose. Thank you for this.

Fearing the unknown

Lord, I'm in hospital and the cause of my being here is still a mystery. Tests—a long stay—a short stay—an operation? I'm in the dark. Is it serious? Is it nothing to worry about? I don't know and I'm worried. I think of the family, my job, my other commitments. Oh, my God, what is it? I'm here to find out. May the doctor's skill and equipment be adequate to give an answer. When I hear the verdict let me be able to accept it. Help me to make the most of my life from here on in. Teach me much in these days of the unknown.

Full of regrets

I've got time to lie here and think, Father. It seems as if my past comes rushing back in spurts. Strangely they're about the unpleasant areas of my life. I'm seeing them differently now. Some of the things I did and didn't do have hurt family, friends and strangers only too often. It distresses me when I think of them. Lord, forgive me. Where possible I would like to right those wrongs. Armed with your forgiveness show me how to do something about it even while in here.

A prayer by a patient for relatives

As I lie here, Lord, I'm not thinking about myself all the time. I sense that this hospitalization is tearing my family apart. Perhaps they know more about my condition than I do. Again, they might be just overwhelmed with the most pessimistic outcome. Lord, they may be just facing reality. Some of them are heartbroken. There's little I can do except put on a brave face. I love them, each one, and don't like seeing them this way. You are the God of comfort; come alongside of them just now. They are finding this a heavy load. I plead with you to share it with them. Add patience to their spirits also.

Full of self-pity

My power of concentration seems to have vanished. It should be a good opportunity to meditate and think, especially about you. But I cannot. It's probably the treatment and the constant ward activity. It has been a crisis and I've done a lot of self-pitying. I've concentrated on myself. That's not your way, is it? Forgive me, Lord, and enable me to lift my thoughts beyond myself.

Denying facts

Lord, many people have been around me today. I've told them everything's going fine. I'm believing almost the opposite of what the doctor told me. I'm not facing the facts. I'm hearing what I want to hear. It means that deep down I'm frightened. Lord! "Being brave" is not the answer. Oh! Help me, Father, to understand the implications of my condition. I need to think quietly and to sort myself out. I believe, oh God, your presence will help me to do just this so that I may be best able to help myself, my loved ones and the staff caring for me.

News of discharge

I'm going home, that sounds good. Father God, I'm grateful for this hospital, for all its staff. They've been thoughtful, tender and so willing to help me. Through their treatment and care I'm being discharged. Through them you have provided so much for my recovery. To you I offer my thanks. Such praise will seem hollow if I do not seek to love and help my neighbor more than I did before. May such a love overflow my life in service to others as I am able.

Recognizing blessing

Hospitalization isn't the best experience, Lord. I find it hard to take the pain, I don't like it. Yet you have known pain too. When I think of the sufferings of Jesus, it makes me feel ashamed. I want to love you more and this hospital experience is helping me do it. I'm beginning to realize that hospitalization can bring its blessing. Please help me discover more of this blessing. You work in wonderful ways.

Improving

It's great to be alive. I didn't think that last week. Each day I'm getting stronger. The old pain has gone. It's wonderful. I'm beginning to make plans for what I'll do when I get home—happy thought. I sense a danger here. I'm likely to become too self-indulgent and demanding. You've stood by me and given me strength during these days of illness. When I've been depressed, angry, irritable, frustrated or anxious, you've been around. Turn my thoughts and plans, oh Lord, to things positive and helpful. I've received much. May I start reaching out to others also.

An uncertain diagnosis

Father, this whole illness of mine is quite mystifying. The doctors are puzzled. They can't tell me what the problem is. To date tests are inconclusive. I'm up in the air. Sometimes I'm full of high hopes; other times I'm pessimistic and fed up with myself. Some would say that I've lost my faith. It's not that, Lord. It is just the impatience of uncertainty. I know that you'll see me through. I know with your help I'll cope, whatever they discover. Your strength will be my strength, your courage, your love will be my confidence until we meet face to face at the appropriate time.

When overwhelmed by weakness

I'm just lying here, Lord, just feeling all-in. It's hard to raise a smile when staff or visitors come. It's an effort to lift my arms. My legs feel like pieces of lead. My mind would have difficulty even in working out the date. My concentration has gone. I want to talk with you. I start, then I drift off. I just can't help it, Lord. You know how it is and I am so grateful you are an understanding God. In my weakness I raise my plea to you. Look upon me, now. Assure me of your continuing love. Touch my weak body, mind and spirit with your spirit, as I struggle with the doctors' help to come out on top of my illness. Give me relaxation now which will promote the healing I need.

Thanksgiving for a new baby

I can't believe it, Lord! We have a brand-new baby. I know I'm prejudiced, my baby's beautiful. My heart is just overflowing with joy. I do want to say thank you for being with us through the pregnancy. It is never easy but your help and strength comforted and supported us all the way. This new life gives us new and greater responsibilities. We have to guide and lead this little life into adulthood. In these days it is an awsome responsibility. As we thank you for our addition to the family, so we cry to you in a different way. Give us wisdom and understanding to be the best parents possible. May our child grow up to recognize and worship you as God and Savior.

For a sick child

My heart and mind, my emotions and thinking are jumbled and confused. My child is ill, close to death. My children are my most priceless possessions. Harm them and you harm me. The doctors are doing their best. The nurses are marvelous. The therapists are excellent and gentle. I couldn't ask for better attention. Yet there is one thing more I need. It is you, oh Lord. Come and hear my prayer. Save my child. May your soothing spirit come upon my child's body, giving peace and your life deep within. In my helplessness I cling to you and plead with you for my child. Hear my cries—mend my shattered heart—calm my tormented mind—may your peace find its place in my breast.

Cry for help

Oh, God, my Lord, I am beyond what I feel I can stand. Help me in what lies ahead. Strengthen my faith in you and myself. Give me confidence in those who are caring for me. Forgive me. Let your peace grow in me, your love comfort me and your presence encourage me.

A midday prayer

The day is half-gone, Lord. I've dozed, I've seen the doctor. I have no energy, I can't think. Time is just idling by. It is so unlike me and I don't like it. Oh, Father, help me to see something positive for my stay here. I pray that the doctors may give me the right treatment. I do want you to strengthen me in body, mind and spirit. Come close to me and bless me with your calming, peaceful presence.

Before special treatment

I'm to commence special treatment today, Lord. Will it help me? Will I have side reactions? The doctors have said that it should be successful. I pray that it may be. I look forward to being rid of sickness and weakness. Today I have a great hope that I may be healed. Give me a new picture of a better and more useful life after this treatment. This is possible, oh my God! if we can tread the days ahead together.

A prayer by relatives for the patient

It's difficult to sit by and watch like this. I willingly would swap places but that's not the way it is. I do pray that pain may be eased. I don't know how best to pray. Do give relief, Lord. I pray that my love may be evident. Let me speak with more than lips. My touch, my presence, my eyes, my tone of voice—let them all echo my love, assurance, and peace that his/her days of illness may be an experience of my support and comfort. Above all, Oh Lord, may he/she turn to you for spiritual strength for all needs.

Rewrite these personal prayers, expressing the patient's own feelings, as your prayer offered on behalf of the patient. This is an important exercise to develop your ability to pray an "incarnational prayer."

Examples of Visitors' Prayers

In the hours before death (for an active believer)

Thank you, Lord, for *name* and his/her hope in you. We thank you for all *name* has meant to so many people. At this moment when *name* waits for the call into your presence, we pray that he/she may be filled with your spirit. May the comfortable feeling of your love and peace fill *name*. May the two of you feel the closeness of each other as your blessing rests upon *name*.

In the hours before death (for a person generally disinterested in religion)

Father, at this time when *name* faces the un-known, we pray that *name* may reach out to you, your spirit reaching down, his/her spirit reaching up until you both find each other. Even in the final hours (days) upon earth may *name* discover an intimacy and peacefulness not experienced before. We pray, Lord God, for the warmth of your presence to settle upon *name* as he/she discovers you in greater truth. May such peace and blessing be *name*'s for eternity.

With angry patient (a)
(an amputee after an accident)

Dear Lord God, you seem so high, mighty and far away from *name* just now. He's only young. He's just starting out to know and understand what life is all about. Now, he's lost a leg and a hand. He is angry with you and depressed. *Name* feels you could have protected him better. Help him to express that anger to you in his own words. He needs to be honest with you. I pray for him, Lord, that you two will understand each other and that *name* with your help will fight his way to the top. Give him courage and determination and a trust in you, in Jesus' name.

For another angry patient (b)

Lord! *Name* has every right to feel angry at what has happened. *Name* has a lot of living to do yet. He/she has dreams and plans to fulfill. It looks as if they are all smashed to pieces. It is not fair. It doesn't seem right. *Name* would like to call you a few names. He/she thinks you could have stopped it. Accept *name*'s anger in all its strength. Be patient and understanding with *name* just now. I want to leave *name* in your care. Be gentle and kind to *name* at this time. Amen.

N.B. To go beyond this in prayer in these circumstances, when God appears to the patient to be unfeeling, would stimulate anger against you.

For an active Christian fighting to live

Name has often expressed anticipation at the great joy of meeting you face-to-face. The race has been faithfully run. Crown *name* with this greatest blessing of all. *Name* is waiting to hear your call. We give *name* the freedom to let go and be with you. We commend his/her spirit to your love. We thank you for *name*, for the love and blessing received by many throughout his/her life. Accept *name*, O Father, in Jesus' name.

N.B. The name of the person is frequently used in these prayers. It reinforces in the patient's mind (often short in concentration) that this prayer is for her or him and thus concentration is kept active. Any feeling of abandonment is dispelled.

Jesus—A Theological Model

A theology of acceptance

Name the type of people you find hard to minister to.

What are some of the traits that turn you off people?

What needs to happen for you to be able to accept them?

Are there times when confrontation and withdrawal are necessary? (Cite examples from your own and Jesus' ministry.)

A theology of availability

Being called out of hours or when you are about to go home—what does it do to you?

Can availability lead to burnout?

Have you a fear of burnout?

Availability may be the tool to lever a pastoral worker into being overused. How would you avoid this?

A theology of accountability

Clergy and pastoral carers are generally individualists and freelancers. We develop our own strategies and methods of working. What criteria can your group list as ways of measuring accountability?

Quality of care, number of people offered care and self-care are the three elements of accountability.

In a scale of 10, set out your priorities for these three. (e.g. quality of care 7, number of People 2, self-care 1.)

A theology of care

From Jesus' ministry and his parables, we hear his call to see the caring ministry through to completion. In an institution it is difficult to follow up.

How concerned are you to ensure an ongoing ministry? What are the factors that make referral back to the community difficult?

How have you handled negative responses from patient, resident or relatives in the past?

How often does duty or responsibility cloud your sense of caring?

A theology of sensitivity

To see, to perceive, to read between the lines when a person is in crisis behavior is evidence of sensitivity.

Are there experiences in your own life that enable you to be more sensitive? (See, e.g., Nouwen's *The Wounded Healer*).

Patronizing and caring are unrelated in quality.

To what degree are you aware of it when you become patronizing?

Discuss the evidence of patronizing behavior.

In what ways may sensitivity skills be sharpened?

A theology of obedience

The success of Jesus' ministry hinged upon his obedience to the call to be the Messiah. It is easy to make excuses as a carer and avoid certain awkward situations or to allow some personal activity to encroach upon our obedience to a challenge or to just routine ministry.

The gifts for pastoral care have been given to be used in obedience to the call and appointment. Sometimes appointments are made without there being evidence of a strong sense of call.

Examine the reality of your call to pastoral care service. To what extent do your own feelings or personal desires interfere with or disrupt your obedient (conscientious) functioning as a pastoral person?

A theology of witness

The obligation to witness is binding upon the followers of Jesus. In the hospital setting fulfilling the role of being "salt" or "light" has significant differences for each type of patient.

Identify and evaluate the effectiveness of your perceptions of witness in your hospital ministry.

A theology of servanthood

Service and servanthood are repeated themes in Christian circles. Church members see the minister as their servant without any serious consideration of their own servanthood.

A sense of service or servanthood may be in stark contrast to your fellow professionals' attitude to their work. Have you experienced friction in the team because of your attitude to your involvement?

A servant philosophy may lead to a pastoral carer being exploited by other staff. Is there a point when the carer begins to limit willingness?

When does team harmony versus patient or resident well-being become an issue to be faced?

Is this a spiritual or merely an ethical issue?

A theology of love

The one word that is eminently Christian is the word "love." Hospital care is a ministry of caring through love and sharing God's love in Christ.

In your contact with some of the seemingly unlovable characters of this world, how are you able to overcome any prejudice you may recognize in yourself?

Discuss the quality, depth and significance of caring love.

Share your concerns about underinvolvement and the possibilities of overinvolvement in particular relationships.

A theology of confrontation

Confrontation, at times, results in broken relationships, misunderstandings and animosity. Confrontation need not have disastrous consequences. Confrontation can be for the good.

Are you too confrontational? In what ways can you control and soften your urge to rush in and confront?

Your passiveness binds you, preventing you from confronting people. List several opportunities you have lost when confrontation was necessary. Write down possible conversations that have been successful in each case and discuss these with other workers.

A theology of renewal

The current popular cry is "Who Cares for the Carers?"

In most cases the carers are left to care for themselves. Self-care in reality is based on self-motivation for renewal. True renewal allows time and space for physical, emotional and spiritual re-creation in appropriate measure.

What are your methods for achieving your physical, emotional and spiritual renewal?

The means of spiritual renewal vary from person to person. Our needs, our personality, our mental and spiritual abilities differ greatly.

Share both your unsuccessful and your successful attempts at renewal.

→ BIBLIOGRAPHY ←

Bonhoeffer, Dietrich. *Life Together: The Classic Exploration of Faith in Community.* London: SCM Press, 1954.

Dobihal, Edward F., Jr., and Charles W. Stewart. *When a Friend Is Dying: A Guide to Caring for the Terminally Ill and Bereaved.* Nashville: Abingdon, 1984.

Harlem, Ole K. *Communication in Medicine: A Challenge to the Profession.* Basel: Karger, 1977.

Irion, Paul E. *Hospice and Ministry.* Nashville: Abingdon, 1988.

Kubler-Ross, Elisabeth. *On Death and Dying: What the Dying Have to Teach Doctors, Nurses, Clergy, and Their Own Families.* New York: Macmillan, 1969.

Lake, Frank. *Clinical Theology: A Theological Psychological Basis to Clinical Pastoral Care.* Abr by Martin Yeomans. London: Darton, Longman and Todd, 1986.

Perry, Lloyd M., and Charles M. Sell. *Speaking to Life's Problems.* Chicago: Moody, 1983.

Richmond, Kent D. *Preaching to Sufferers: God and the Problem of Pain.* Nashville: Abingdon, 1988.

Soulen, Richard N., et al. *Care for the Dying.* (Atlanta: Westminster John Knox) 1978.

Zima, Joseph P. *Interviewing: Key to Effective Management.* Chicago: Scientific Research Associates, 1981.